AS GOOD AS DEAD

True Stories from Wasilla, Alaska

Printed in the United States of America

Table of Contents

DEDICATION

To those who've had close calls with death, have ever found themselves in despair or are simply seeking to live a better life, this book is dedicated to you!

And to all the people, like the seven from Wasilla you'll meet in these pages, whose courage and transparency in sharing their stories can be a beacon of hope to anyone who may have felt that their lives were *As Good As Dead.*

ACKNOWLEDGEMENTS

I would like to thank Dennis Hotchkiss for his vision for this book and Ruben Reyes for his hard work in making it a reality. And to the people of Northgate Alaska, thank you for your boldness and vulnerability in sharing your personal stories.

This book would not have been published without the amazing efforts of our project manager and editor, Hayley Pandolph. Her untiring resolve pushed this project forward and turned it into a stunning victory. Thank you for your great fortitude and diligence. Deep thanks to our incredible Editor in Chief, Michelle Cuthrell, and Executive Editor, Jen Genovesi, for all the amazing work they do. I would also like to thank our invaluable proofreader, Melody Davis, for the focus and energy she has put into perfecting our words.

Lastly, I want to extend our gratitude to the creative and very talented Jenny Randle, who designed the beautiful cover for *As Good As Dead: True Stories from Wasilla, Alaska.*

Daren Lindley
President and CEO
Good Catch Publishing

The book you are about to read
is a compilation of authentic life stories.
The facts are true, and the events are real.
These storytellers have dealt with crisis, tragedy, abuse
and neglect and have shared their most private moments,
mess-ups and hang-ups in order for others to learn and
grow from them. In order to protect the identities of those
involved in their pasts, the names and details of some
storytellers have been withheld or changed.

INTRODUCTION

What do you do when life is careening out of control? When addiction has overtaken you or abuse chained you with fear? Is depression escapable? Will relationships ever be healthy again? Are we destined to dissolve into an abyss of sorrow? Or will the sunlight of happiness ever return?

Your life really can change. It is possible to become a new person. The seven stories you are about to read prove positively that people right here in our town have stopped dying and started living. Whether they've been beaten down by abuse, broken promises, shattered dreams or suffocating addictions, the resounding answer is, "Yes! You can become a new person." The potential to break free from gloom and into a bright future awaits.

Expect inspiration, hope and transformation! As you walk with these real people from our very own city through the pages of this book, you will not only find riveting accounts of their hardships; you will learn the secrets that brought about their breakthroughs. These people are no longer living in the shadows of yesterday. They are thriving with a sense of mission and purpose TODAY. May these stories inspire you to do the same.

TERROR ON THE GLASS
The Story of Rodney
Written by Richard Drebert

I loved the snow in Alaska.

White on a mirror, my razor blade caressed its powdery drifts, and I watched my beloved Sonja breathe it in, her dark eyelashes fluttering.

She waited for the cocaine to cut a path to her brain, and soon she would fly, leaving her problems behind. Confident, mentally agile for hours at a time, Sonja and I often soared high above the humdrum world, like wild ravens.

In our hippie culture I was known as Doc. Whatever ailed your cannabis, I could help you find the cure, and I mentored friends in exploring paths that often led them to harder drugs. Pot was a suicidal gateway.

Our first summer together, I tried to help my Sonja find bliss in marijuana, but it was coke that hooked her. I told myself that I was sharing my heart with her. The pot plants I pampered, the cocaine I bought and sold, wasn't just product to me — it was my identity.

Marijuana calmed me, softening the sharp traumas I carried from childhood — but cocaine rewired my personality. A close friend of mine had helped me snort my first line of cocaine, too, and I had awakened to unmatched sensory pleasures, while a seething darkness invaded my soul.

And the darkness was *alive.*

❧❧❧

I realize now that witnessing a fiery tragedy when I was 3 years old trenched a wound in my formative psyche.

I loved watching the airplanes droning above laughing children in the Pacoima school yard across the street from our house — but one afternoon two planes met in midair over the playground ...

After the air collision in 1957, my nerves never seemed to heal. I spent most of my untamed youth tranquilizing a nameless trauma inside me, and my dysfunctional family inflamed the pain.

I remember my father as a functional alcoholic Catholic. My mother was a devout Catholic — and among us nine kids, I was a *confused* Catholic. Growing up in Pacoima, California, I was shy, introverted and carried a strange dread of the world around with me.

My one and only year of Catholic school convinced me that I could never measure up to the rules the nuns enforced for God. I believed that no mercy existed to deliver me from the torment waiting for me in purgatory, and I quaked over my certain doom.

When I was in fourth grade, Dad moved us away from

the street gangs that encroached on every major street corner in Pacoima. He built a dream home — from footings to shingles — on the outskirts of Los Angeles.

Our wonderful new neighborhood distracted me from my angst for a few years. Mom herded us to Catholic church every week without fail, and our family seemed destined to become an upper-middle-class family. I explored new territory and swam in backyard swimming pools with our new friends.

Then one night Dad came home drunk and dispirited. He cursed and spluttered the names of two businessmen we all knew he was working for. He stomped back and forth on his hardwood floors, raging: "They owe me! They owe me thousands!"

My father had remodeled their opulent homes, but his shrewd clients found a way to cheat him out of construction wages and material costs. The California economy was soft in the '60s, and Dad's small company suddenly teetered at the edge of financial ruin. In a few months, foreclosure letters piled up. Dad stumbled home drunk night after night, blistering the air with angry, irrational tirades — now targeting my mother.

One day, my older brother got crossways with the law and agreed to leave the state to avoid prosecution. Dad decided to use this excuse to make his escape with my brother, and he loaded up his pickup and headed up the Alaska-Canadian Highway. The '64 earthquake had leveled hundreds of structures in Alaska, and carpenters were in short supply.

My mother breathed a sigh of relief when he left, and I did, too.

Mom's cousin, a Catholic missionary to Chile whom I called Father Fred, showed up for a visit while we were packing up to vacate our foreclosed dream home. Mom's parents had invited us back to their 160-acre family farm in Minnesota to start a new life, and we had sold most of our possessions.

Our '63 Bel Air station wagon barely held all nine of us — but Father Fred, with his priestly collar and big grin, squeezed in, too. He and Mom shared the driving chores as we ambled cross-country through the Midwest.

Road games and lightning storms cast a happy glow on our trip to Sebeka, Minnesota. Dad's fury and failures were behind us, and Mom was happier than we had seen her in years. After days of travel, jovial Father Fred pointed out Holstein cows and horses grazing contentedly in green pastures. I sat in our rolling sardine can wishing I could sit next to *them* and absorb the peace and quiet. City noise and hustle and bustle seemed foreign here. In hay meadows I felt like I might find the peace I craved.

As we piled out of the Bel Air at the farm, Mom's brothers and sisters, her mother and father and dozens of my cousins surrounded us like a goose down comforter. My grandparents — retired farmers — lived on the home place. They were loving family icons, and around them, dairy farms and cornfields were organized like a checkerboard, owned by my uncles and aunts.

TERROR ON THE GLASS

Grandpa and Grandma moved our whole family into a vacant farmhouse, and in the mornings before chores we washed down Mom's biscuits with milk fresh from cows we grew to know by name.

No one among my 50 cousins would have considered missing Catholic Mass, and they all worked as hard as the adults. I adapted to weeding gardens, churning butter, riding horses, feeding stock and running *wild*. I was born for country life! For almost a year I romped and worked on Grandpa's farm — planning on enrolling in school — until Dad's pickup growled down Grandpa's long gravel driveway one evening. He had it all planned: He was moving his family to Alaska.

As I listened to Mom and Dad argue in the farmhouse, my old fears and inner turmoil weighed on me like heavy sacks of oats. My mother and us kids were slaves to my father's decision.

On the way to Alaska, I sat in the back seat of our Bel Air, mesmerized by the incessant tire vibration on the gravel highway. I breathed through a blanket to filter out the road dust and Dad's cigarette smoke. The 11 of us had left the family farm in a muddle of tears and bitterness. Mom's family didn't try to hide their contempt for Dad's drinking and verbal abuse, but they couldn't convince Mom to stay in Minnesota.

Mom took her marriage vows seriously. She dutifully loaded our station wagon for an Alaskan odyssey — praying that God would keep us safe. Her calm inner strength usually impressed me during these upheavals, inviting me to explore where it originated. But on our trip north, while Dad puffed contentedly on coffin nails, I felt only anger at leaving our security behind. I had hundreds of miles to worry about our uncertain future.

☙☙☙

One main artery bisected Wasilla, Alaska, and if you shot clear through it, you'd be traveling remote stretches of wilderness to Fairbanks 300 miles north. Dad offloaded us at the Willowa Resort (with a convenient bar), where Mom stacked us like cordwood into a couple rented rooms. When Dad's carpentry work fizzled out, Mom tossed our clothes in the Bel Air again, and we drove to a burg even smaller than Wasilla. In the community called "Big Lake," Dad swung a hammer again, while Mom and us kids tried to keep sane in tiny cabin rooms.

Then one day Dad flung the door open with a big grin.

"I got a surprise for you! We're moving to a real homestead. Forty acres and a fish pond!"

What he didn't say was that we boys had to buck firewood with a Swede saw to heat the dilapidated old house. Our new digs had a phone and electricity, but I had to ride a bus 15 miles to school in Wasilla every day.

Our first winter in Alaska my dad helped my brother and me get jobs patrolling upscale waterfront cabins on frozen Rocky Lake nearby. We shoveled roofs and decks to fool thieves into believing that they were lived in. When summer finally arrived, I spent much of the time at Fish Creek, hauling in good-sized trout for the dinner table.

When Dad's job at Big Lake petered out, we moved back to Wasilla.

After we finally settled into a house we could afford, I discovered an ability that satisfied my yearning to *create* harmony where none existed in our otherwise chaotic lives. I played guitar, mimicking musicians like the Beach Boys and the Beatles — but I wanted to go beyond strumming chords. To find the soul in my music, I *built* my first guitar, and the seed of a luthier (stringed instrument craftsman) began to grow. During my drug-sick years it should have shriveled, but the seed was protected by a patient mentor I had yet to meet.

In ninth grade I landed a job with a youth organization, pulling weeds and brushing out trails around parks. With my first checks I saved up enough money to buy a Honda 50 motorcycle, and suddenly, I sprang free from the family trap! Exhilarating! I wove in and out of traffic, grazing bumpers and racing across old homestead trails with abandon. I had been bound up in everyone else's dreams, but never again.

I wanted to try everything, and the hippie culture sucked me in like a leech to a vein. Cigarettes and pool games led to new friendships, and parties led me to experimenting with marijuana and psychedelic drugs. I still bunked with my little brothers, and I couldn't wait to move away.

Dad drank more than ever, and when he was home he

still dragged himself out of bed to attend Catholic church with Mom. Twisted strands of religion bound our family together — care-worn and dog-eared — and each strand snapped as we children left the nest for good.

Mom seemed to be the only one who had a relationship with this Jesus we heard about in church — and her prayers for my safety were answered. I should have been mangled over and over, as often as I lurched recklessly through intersections high on pot or LSD.

Mom never gave up hope that I might relent and become a Catholic priest someday — her dream, NOT mine. As for my father, he left religion at the door of his favorite tavern before he bellied up to the bar. Never measuring up to the rules in God's approved church on earth had set my dad on a trail of hopelessness, too — like father, like son.

Then, one fateful day, like falling through lake ice, I plunged into bone-chilling truth: Not even drugs could ease the grief over the death of a close friend.

అలా అలా అలా

Joe should have been a graduating senior when the train killed him on the Wasilla Highway, but he had dropped out of school. Joe was my best stoner friend in the world.

I stood like a statue, my mouth agape, when Mom told me that she had driven past the scene of an accident where

Joe's mutilated 350 Honda Scrambler lay near the railroad tracks. Alaska Railroad cars were frozen in red tape for hours, until the investigation was over.

No one knew exactly what happened, but I pictured Joe challenging the train to a game of chicken, hitting a familiar pothole and losing control. In fact, I was seeing a lot more than the accident in my mind. The blue and yellow train slithered like sections of a massive toy snake, and I shook my head to refocus on Mom and my crying sisters. I made my way to my bedroom, hoping no one noticed that I was high.

I was new to this mushroom derivative, and my best friend's death made coming down all the *harder.*

A sad vision of my friend's blood smeared on the railroad tracks showed brightly in my mind, but my drug trip was plugging up my emotions.

Later, I thought. *Maybe later tears will come …*

I graduated from high school the year after Joe died. It was the same year that I moved into a pad with other stoners. It was the same year that I decided psychedelic drugs were too hard-edged and intense for me. I partook of mushrooms sporadically, but marijuana became my misty elixir, my savior. It deadened my senses to insecurity and fear. Nothing could find me in the warm fog of marijuana. I was invisible — even to myself.

One particularly scary trip on LSD had reinforced my dedication to pot — I awoke to reality clinging to the wispy top of a tall spruce tree. At the time I lived in a cabin with five other hippies, who sponged off two of us who actually worked to support our habits. After that, I had decided once and for all: No meth. No LSD. *Just weed. It's all I need.* And I stuck to my mantra through the next few years, living a daily pot "maintenance" lifestyle.

In junior high, I had encountered the true "soul" in my music by crafting an acoustic guitar. As a young adult I wanted to *know* my cannabis. My best highs were achieved if certain horticulture science was applied before harvesting. I began studying how to create the most potent plants in Alaska.

కికికి

But Dad needed me.

He had taken a job transforming a residence into a commercial building, and he couldn't complete the work alone. It was all I could do to tolerate him berating me, his outbursts of rage and his drinking (rather than eating) his lunches.

When he ran his fingers through the spinning blades of a lumber planer, my fate was sealed. He *really* needed me then. For two months I gritted my teeth and smoked pot to deaden my feelings of hatred and despair. His hand still hadn't healed completely when the job was finished, but I lit out as fast as I could, before he could ask me to help him on any other job.

I found a new vocation working for absent

homeowners, and it allowed me to begin growing my own pot. As a reliable caretaker in the Wasilla area, I seldom got visitors, and I had plenty of time to experiment with lighting and soils inside other peoples' homes.

One day Dad and Mom popped in to say hello ...

When she saw my pot garden, Mom's face fell, like she had lost her best friend. I felt her disappointment in my gut and needed a joint badly.

"Rodney. If you don't get rid of those ... those ... *plants*, I'm calling the police!"

This was the last thing I wanted to hear from my own mother. Dad thought it was funny and grinned at me as she stormed out the door.

This event drove a wedge between Mom and me, and I didn't visit her for months. Dad, on the other hand, warmed up to the *other* addict in the family, and he even smoked weed with me sometimes.

By the next summer, my ambition to grow my own marijuana had reached a new high. For a few months I grew it with a friend, but soon I found a place far off the grid where I could put my expertise to work. I saved money from carpentry jobs until I could buy my own land, and I built a greenhouse that accommodated 15 quality pot plants.

My best buds during this time of my life were my plants. We didn't need anyone else. My marijuana had me to feed them Miracle-Gro, and I had *them* — to fill my lungs every few hours. Kerosene lamps lighted my evenings as I sloughed into a haze of melancholic repose.

What finally drove me from my cave was a need to pay bills, and I emerged with a new plan.

ళళళ

I was the guy that you tell your daughters, "Don't smile back!" when he pulls up beside her at a stoplight.

With stringy, shoulder-length hair, dilated hazel eyes and lanky (almost skeletal), at 6 feet tall, I was the hippie everyone loved to hate. I drove through Wasilla in a Volkswagen van, a peace child whose motto was: *Live and let live, man.*

Whenever we hippies congregated in a tent to pass around a joint and chew the fat, we avoided subjects like religion. The Great Spirit was in everything. In everyone. Church was the Alaska forest, and we attended pot-smoking meetings regularly. It beat the h*** out of Catholic Mass.

Peace came from our dope, and *everyone* needed more peace — so I decided to start selling it. My new venture bloomed quickly, and I joined a sophisticated group of growers who mentored me in budding techniques.

In a short time, growers began seeking me out when they had problems with their plants. I was their Doc, and for the first time in my life, I felt like *somebody*. I began developing a custom strain of high-grade marijuana — potent and in demand.

A fellow grower and friend joined me in experimenting on our green leafy children, but his ambitions ranged farther than mine. He found a supplier of cocaine in Anchorage, and he already knew customers who wanted hard drugs in the outskirts of Wasilla. I tried a little. Then a little more again — and I loved how it created a new me.

When I was high on coke, I had something to say. No more hanging back, holding back. I just said what I thought, and it sounded profound! I felt stimulated, animated.

My old mantra, *Just weed, it's all I need*, went up in smoke.

๛๛๛

Sonja and I grew up in California 10 miles apart, and we didn't even know it.

With an ebony afro, olive complexion and shapely in her Levi's, I couldn't take my eyes off her. She captivated me, and I needed to know more about the woman.

To my utter delight, our attraction was mutual. Her older brother was a good friend of mine, and they had grown up in the same kind of dysfunctional Catholic family as mine. Painfully shy like me, Sonja and I spent a whole summer getting to know one another, until she had to leave for her next semester of nursing classes in California.

I loved Sonja and told her so before she left — but she didn't believe it. She just thought the dope was talking.

When she flew back to California, I was heartbroken

and marijuana only depressed me more, so I turned to a convenient new passion — one that seduced me closer to a nightmare. Pot had opened the door to darkness, and *cocaine* waited to invade my mind.

In the beginning, I thought that I owned my habit. I called myself a "maintenance user" (an addict who plans out his day): snorting coke in the morning; working for a few hours in the real world; more coke and partying with friends in the evening; then smoking pot late to gently drift into oblivion — and do it all over again as often as possible.

Cocaine fundamentally changed my brain. In reality I was a gaunt, long-haired hippie who dodged in and out of conversations like a hopped-up kid on a Honda 50. But after a snort I felt transformed into a suave, confident intellectual — a *cool* individual.

Sometimes a sliver of truth sliced through all the confusion in my mind. I needed something *more.* In lucid moments I felt desolate, like I sat in the back of the old Bel Air again — being driven somewhere I didn't want to go.

And what was waiting for me at the other end of the highway?

I ached to love someone who *really* cared about me, and only one person I knew had shown me tenderness without clamoring after my dope. Sonja still held me captive, and I loved her from afar until it became unbearable to live without her. I had to see her. I had to tell her that I loved her again … I made a trip to California, and this time she believed me.

When Sonja moved back to Alaska and into my custom-built dream home, she enrolled at University of Anchorage and completed her nurse's training program. But rather than altering my dysfunctional lifestyle to accommodate her new career, I absorbed Sonja into mine.

My addiction to cocaine ruled every waking moment, and in time my sweet Sonja climbed the suicidal ladder toward becoming a maintenance user, too. Our weekends always included partying with friends or a quiet evening together — snorting coke.

Paranoia — cocaine's evil twin — took up residence in my mind. Paranoia taunted me about the cops closing in, or about friends who might rat me out, or kill me for my stash.

Finally I told everyone that I no longer grew any pot to sell anymore — an obvious lie, because I never turned anyone away who wanted to buy my product.

I studied coke the way I had pot, and I learned to freebase (alter the form for smoking). I planned to offer this crack cocaine to clients at a higher price, but I needed to experiment first. My new best friend, James, agreed to be a guinea pig with me.

After his first hit, he shook his head. "Nothin'. Don't feel nothin', Rodney …"

My own crack was hitting me between the eyes, and I heaped his pipe, instructing him how to breathe and … suddenly he stood up.

"I gotta get outta here!"

James' eyes were bulging out, and I worried they might

pop out onto the floor. Euphoria never touched James — instead terror drove him out the door. He surrounded a birch tree with his two big arms, chuffing in short, erratic breaths, like he endured horrible pain. He seemed to be *just holding on* until evil stopped violating his soul.

I thought I was killing James.

An hour later, he peeled himself off the tree, still shaking, and I drove him home before Sonja returned from her nightshift at the hospital. Even after this close call, I could sense my craving for this poison intensifying like never before, and I tried to ignore any guilt seeping past my addiction.

My Jesus-freak sister, Anna, had visited, and she tried to talk sense into Sonja and me.

"Give your lives to Jesus. He's the answer to your search for peace. Just pray like this …"

Her words seemed surreal yet serene at the time, and now I wished I could forget them! Jesus freaks reminded me of my future in purgatory.

Soon after Anna's visit, a Bible had arrived in the mail, and Sonja placed my sister's gift on a dresser. For days I avoided this Bible like bad juju.

The night after James OD'd, Sonja was at work, and a group of potential clients came over to score. I gave them a coke sample to reel them in, and they left at about 4 a.m. — with my product. Triumphant with a wad of cash and ramped up too high to sleep, I decided to finish staining some kitchen cabinets to surprise Sonja.

The Varathane fumes stung my eyes. I brushed the

thick liquid inside a cupboard, breathing in, breathing out. Suddenly I stood up and threw my brush down. I craved coke. With shaky fingers, I dumped a line of cocaine onto a smudged piece of mirror.

Exhale … breathe in *hard* …

Thirty minutes later, another line.

Minutes later, again …

Even in my extreme agitation I knew I was under the influence of an entity that wasn't me. A darkness — thick like the Varathane — oozed into my senses, choking me. This darkness was living, hellish, suffocating, and my heart thundered in my ears as I stood close to the edge of eternity. I experienced sheer terror waiting for my brain to shut down for good.

Sonja would be home soon to find my body, stinking, my eyes bulging like James' … I stumbled to the bedroom.

What was it that Anna told us?

I didn't say a word aloud, but in my head I was screaming as I fell onto the bed.

JESUS! Help me! I can't do this anymore. I'm dying. Save me … JESUS!

It seemed ludicrous to expect God to answer me now, after all these years of rejecting him. But I was desperate. I had run out of time.

Suddenly, my sinuses began to *empty.* My nose ran like a faucet as the suffocating, living darkness seemed to be flushed out of me. Every microgram of cocaine excreted away, and the thundering tempest in my chest obeyed a quiet command from Jesus: "Peace. Be still."

Tranquility like I had never experienced enveloped me. This was a peace far greater than what I experienced on the Minnesota farm; far more intense than any hallucinogen; and more satisfying than any acoustic nirvana I had enjoyed while playing or building guitars.

Without drugs and without a priest, I met God.

When I opened Anna's Bible gift, it flopped open to Proverbs 10, and I read the first verse: "… a wise son makes a father glad, but a foolish son is a grief to his mother" (NASB).

Mom had been grieving over me for years, praying for me — and in that moment I finally understood how much she loved me. As I read more of the Bible, a strange soul "flushing" continued as I sorrowfully acknowledged my utter ignorance about God's plan for my life. Every verse in Proverbs 10 revealed the real me: selfish, fear-ridden, angry, full of guilt. I knew that I had to change direction for good.

After about an hour of reading verses and praying for forgiveness, I gathered up thousands of dollars worth of high-grade pot and cocaine — my labor of love, my cherished life investment — and tossed every gram and leaf into the woodstove. In the belly of this iron altar my past life burned away as I promised to follow Jesus the rest of my life.

Then, Sonja came home …

"You *what?*"
"Yup. It's all gone. I gave my life to Jesus, Sonja."

I tried to explain about how God had spared my life after a serious cocaine overdose. She listened intently with a quizzical expression, not certain if I was high and irrational. I told her about the peace I felt and that I was a new man — rewired instantly by Jesus!

Sonja slowly digested the words from this stranger, and then it hit her — it was her weekend to kick back and snort a few lines. She opened the woodstove and sniffed.

"Nice, Rodney, but some of that stuff was *mine*! What am I supposed to do?"

"Babe, you gotta quit, too … it's killing us."

I could see panic welling up in her eyes.

"And, Sonja, we need to get married, too."

Our heart-to-heart talk lasted all morning, until finally Sonja needed more than lunch to help her endure this day of crazy changes. From her very private stash she found a vial of cocaine and cut the powder with infinite care on a mirror.

Perhaps it would have been her last hit forever. Or maybe she *never* would have found the strength to break the chains of addiction had she indulged this last time.

Before she could position her straw, I blew it all away! Her coke was irretrievably *gone*, and she looked at me aghast. "What the h*** is wrong with you?"

"I can't let you do this anymore, hon. I got you onto coke. I'm so sorry. Please, please — *no more.*"

My beloved Sonja glanced at the dust on the floor mingled with snowy white sprinkles and shook her head, resigned and trying to understand.

AS GOOD AS DEAD

❧❧❧

Just a week after I did, Sonja gave her heart to Jesus Christ, too. Five weeks after I burned our dope in the woodstove, I married Sonja — a sweet, godly woman, no longer pining for cocaine to lift her spirits.

To say we cleaned up our act and that we lived happily ever after skips pages and pages of heartaches and joys we have experienced together.

Jesus knew we would struggle in our promises to serve him. That's why he died on the cross to pay for our failures: past, present and future. We learned that the life-altering peace and security we received was a gift of God, completely unearned.

And when I failed Jesus that next summer by snorting coke at a friend's house, it was *Sonja* who laid down the law this time.

"Get clean for good, Rodney, or I'm leaving you."

No contest. I knew that God was speaking loud and clear.

For 33 years, my darling Sonja has been my faithful friend, my children's home school teacher, my partner in ministry. Our three sons are grown men now, and to Sonja's credit, each one is serving Jesus.

My luthier seed — planted by my patient Mentor — is sprouting. I believe that someday my dream of building musical instruments as a family business may be realized.

In God's time I want to help other young people find the soul in their music as I have.

God has led Sonja and me to Northgate Alaska church, to serve with our loving friends. No two guitars sound alike, and among these friends, our ministries resonate with unique sounds, too.

Sometimes I drift back to my childhood and recall events that trenched deep furrows of despair in my life, until Jesus lifted me onto his way …

I stood in our backyard in Pacoima, staring toward the roar of plane engines. Aircraft came and went from an airport not far away, and I often watched them as they droned above the grade school across the street from our house.

A private plane and a vintage WWII bomber with gun turrets and USAF painted on its fuselage slowly entered the airspace above the school for a few seconds — before colliding. A frightening ball of flame seared my little mind, as, transfixed, I watched burning wings, engine pieces and what must have been body parts spreading like shrapnel over the school yard. I heard hunks of the airplanes striking pavement. I heard children screaming.

It was months before my mother could coax me out of the house without struggling.

The trauma of that scene stalked me for years — until the moment that I gave my heart to God. The childhood terror drained away on the day I trusted my future to Jesus Christ.

Peace has replaced every trauma once and for all.

THE GIRL IN THE MIRROR

The Story of Angel

Written by Karen Koczwara

I can't breathe.

My throat constricts as the cheap gas station pastries I devoured minutes ago now lodge against my insides. I begin choking, remnants of the dry sugary substance still lingering on my tongue. I gasp for air, but I only choke more. Panic seizes me as I realize I am all alone and I cannot breathe.

I gasp for air again, and at last, it comes. Relief washes over me as I gulp a deep breath as though it is my first and last. Tears prick my eyes as I glance down at the toilet below, where bits of pastry float. I am instantly filled with disgust — disgust for myself and the fact that I have nearly choked to death on something I loathe. I quickly flush the toilet and watch as the water swirls and washes away the evidence of my dark, painful secret.

Suddenly weak, I struggle to stand up. But to my horror, the toilet water rises and spills out the sides of the porcelain bowl. I shriek and jump back, but it's too late. Nasty sewage spews onto the ground and covers my feet, snaking around me in a pool of filth. I watch helplessly as it keeps on coming. I am entrenched by the very thing I've tried to flush away.

I am standing in my own worst nightmare, and I hate myself. I hate the burn that rips through me as I purge my food, but more, I hate the pain that eats at my heart. The tears flow as I sit in the mess, the contents reminiscent of the way I feel inside. Worthless. Ugly. Disgusting.

"I can't do this anymore!" I cry.

I know what rock bottom feels like, because I've reached it right now.

৵৵৵

I was a child of the '70s, the era of bell bottoms, big hair and disco fever. When I was 3 years old, my father moved our family from Texas to Alaska for his work. We settled into a small one-story home in a modest neighborhood.

My beginnings were nothing extraordinary. My parents were loving, and my home felt safe. But things were about to change.

When I was 4 years old, we got a new babysitter. I didn't like her at all. She tried to stuff me into my doll's high chair, despite my protests that I was too big. When the chair broke, she grew angry, and I grew upset. She then threatened to take me outside naked if I did not obey her.

"Please don't make her babysit me anymore!" I begged my mother. "She's mean and treats me like a baby!"

"Now, Angel, you're just being dramatic," my mother replied, smiling.

It was true that I could be dramatic. But even my sister could see how poorly my sitter treated me. My little stomach clenched every time she showed up at the door.

One day, my sitter grew impatient when I did not do what she wanted. She promptly dragged me outside by my hair and paraded me around the neighborhood on my little bike. Cold and embarrassed, I began to whimper and cry.

The neighbors saw what was happening and called my mother. Shortly after, I found her crying on the couch. I had never seen her so distraught and emotional — what was going on? Few words were spoken about it after that, but my sitter never returned.

When I was 5 years old, a teenage family friend came to visit. He encouraged me to hide in my closet and then shoved his tongue in my mouth. I pulled back, disgusted by his saliva against mine. I didn't know the first thing about kissing boys, but I knew I didn't like this one bit.

One night, when I was 6 years old, I had trouble falling asleep. My mother had returned to school in the evenings, leaving my father home alone to care for us. I slipped out of bed and padded down the hall, where a light flickered in the living room. As I peered around the corner, I was shocked to see my father sitting on the sofa watching naked people on TV. I gasped inwardly, horrified by the images portrayed on the screen. My father — a prominent man in the church our family attended — was secretly watching naughty movies! Disgusted, I slipped back into my room and went to bed. But when I closed my eyes, the images were still there, haunting me as I drifted off to sleep.

My parents took us to church each Sunday, and I enjoyed going. When I was 8 years old, a man came to speak at our church. He talked about how each of us could make the decision to have a personal relationship with God by inviting him into our heart. I liked the idea of having God as my best friend, someone I could talk to if I felt scared, confused or alone. During a gathering one night, I felt something stir in my heart. I wanted to go forward to talk with the pastor about God, but I wasn't quite ready yet.

"I want to ask Jesus into my heart, but I need to pick out the right outfit first," I told my parents.

They smiled at me, amused. "That's great, Angel," they said. "What do you think you will wear?"

I opted for my cowboy boots, which I wore proudly as I made my way down the aisle the next time we went to church. I bowed my head and asked Jesus if he would come into my heart and life. I half expected to feel different somehow as I shuffled back to my seat, but I was still the same little girl in her favorite cowboy boots when I sat down.

We moved to a new town when I was in the third grade. I liked school well enough, and I made a best friend. We spent time together giggling and sharing secrets as little girls do. Life resumed a steady, predictable pace — church on Sundays, school on weekdays, with plenty of time for play in between.

THE GIRL IN THE MIRROR

As I entered my junior high and high school years, I threw myself into my studies and extracurricular activities. I had plenty of friends, but a certain loneliness nagged at me, carving a small hole inside. Despite being surrounded by people at home, church and school, I often felt alone. At times, I even felt like an outsider among my own family members. I had everything going for me, so why did I feel so isolated and insecure?

When I was 16, I attended a youth conference at church. Up until then, I had attended church faithfully, but having a relationship with God hadn't meant much to me. Though my parents were active in the church, we rarely talked about God in our everyday lives. But during the conference, something shifted in me. Glancing around, I was inspired to see such a large, diverse group of kids coming together. I suddenly realized that I wanted more. I didn't want to simply learn about God; I wanted to really know him. The speakers shared their own stories and encouraged us to pursue God with our whole heart. By doing so, we could truly experience a peace and joy we would not find anywhere else in life.

I began praying, talking to God just as I would a good friend. I shared everything that was on my heart, from my fears to my triumphs and everything in between. The more I prayed, the easier it became. I loved knowing that no matter where I was, I could come to God day or night and pour out my heart to him. And slowly, I began to realize that despite feeling lonely much of the time, if I relied on God, I'd never truly be alone.

Despite my growing relationship with God, my insecurities still plagued me. When I learned I had to give a speech in front of my class one day, I decided to skip school. The idea of speaking in front of my peers was terrifying — what if I screwed up and they mocked me? Even when I was nominated for homecoming court, my nerves got the best of me. I hated being in the spotlight. *No one really knows me,* I thought sadly. *They don't see the scared, lonely girl beneath the smile.*

One morning, when I was 17, I awoke with an overwhelming feeling of dread. As I dragged my feet out of bed, the cloud of depression that had followed me for so long seemed so thick I could not escape it. I remembered my father's gun collection in the other room. On impulse, I grabbed one of his guns and slipped outside and into the nearby woods. My pulse quickened as my feet trampled the earth below. I was a year away from graduation, with my entire future ahead of me. Yet life no longer felt worth living anymore. I tightened my knuckles around the gun, reminding myself that I could snuff out my life with one pull of the trigger. One bullet and I could be dead. No more pain. No more loneliness.

The sun peeked over the rugged Alaskan mountains, beckoning a new day. It was a beautiful morning, but I noticed none of my surroundings. Instead, I dug my feet into the ground and fingered the gun, wondering how it would feel to die. Would it be quick? Would I feel pain? Would anyone notice I was gone?

My heart raced faster as I considered the option.

Suicide. It would be so easy. Yet something held me back, kept me from pulling the trigger. What was it exactly? God? My family? The notion that perhaps I really did want to live? After several minutes of standing in the woods with that gun in my trembling hands, I dropped it to the ground and ran back to the house. I eased myself into a living room chair and waited for my mother to wake up.

At last, my mother entered the room, rubbing the sleep from her eyes. I sucked in my breath, hoping she might ask if I was okay or why I was not getting ready for school. But instead she just mumbled hello and went about her morning routine. My heart sank. If only she knew I was about to kill myself in the woods moments ago. Slowly, I pulled myself from the chair and proceeded to get ready for school. It would be another ordinary day, yet it could have been the last day of my life.

My senior year, a boy named Raul came to my school. He had recently moved from another city, and I found him especially charismatic and charming. We began hanging out, but my friends disapproved of our relationship.

"I don't like that dude," one of my guy friends told me. "He seems like bad news."

I laughed off his warning. "Raul? He's cool. You just don't know him like I do," I said in his defense.

Raul and I began dating, and I was elated. I loved our deep conversations and felt I could share my heart openly with him. I told him about my suicidal moment, and he confessed that his father was an alcoholic. At last, I thought, I'd found someone who truly understood me.

Raul told me he had invited Jesus into his life shortly before he moved to our town. He said he still had much to learn about God, but I was happy that we shared the same faith.

The following year, when I was just 19 years old, Raul and I married. I knew we were young, but I didn't care. We would find a way to defy the odds and make our life together work. I was a virgin when we married, and I was happy to give myself to Raul, the first guy I had truly ever loved.

Several months after we married, I learned I was pregnant. I gave birth to a healthy baby boy, and for a while, it seemed all the pieces of my life were finally coming together. I had a loving husband who understood me, a child of my own and an entire future ahead of us. But little did I know a storm was about to hit, and it would threaten to rip our happy home to shreds.

❧ ❧ ❧

I held the video between shaking hands, suddenly sick to my stomach over my discovery. My new husband had a secret porn stash — unbelievable. Raul was gone but would be back soon. I'd waste no time confronting him.

The minute Raul walked in the door, I charged toward him, waving the video in the air.

"What do you have to say about this?" I demanded,

shoving it in his face. "How long have you been watching porn, huh?"

Raul held up his hand. "Cool it, okay? It's not a big deal, Angel, all right? Every guy watches a little porn now and then."

"Oh, really? Well, I thought you weren't every guy." I stormed off, holding back angry tears. I'd been so sure Raul was different. How could he do this to me? I already struggled with my self-esteem as it was. The last thing I needed was him watching extremely graphic porn videos and lusting over naked women.

One afternoon, not long after I found the video, I stumbled upon a porn magazine stash while visiting my father. Immediately, my mind went to when I was 6, walking in on my father watching bad movies. *Not you, too, Dad!* My heart sank at the idea that both my husband and father, men who claimed to have integrity, were covering up a filthy habit.

A short time after my second discovery, my sister-in-law approached me with yet another confession. "Your brother has a porn problem, and I don't know what to do about it," she said grimly.

I felt like I'd just been beaten over the head with a boulder. Was every guy on the planet a liar? Did every male have a dirty mind? I was disgusted beyond words, but worse, I was plain disappointed. How could I trust my husband and the other men in my life again?

I was often hopeful that our marriage would improve, but instead, things only took a turn for the worse. Many nights, Raul headed out to the bars with his friends, not bothering to come home until 3 a.m.

"Where were you last night?" I demanded when he finally awoke the next morning.

"Out. I told you I was going out," he mumbled, avoiding eye contact.

"Yeah, well, you've been out almost every day this week," I snapped. "Did you remember you have a wife and kid at home?"

I learned I was pregnant with our second child. While I was thrilled about the baby, I wasn't happy about the way things were going in my marriage. Raul continued to watch porn and wave his problem away, saying I was overreacting. He agreed to see a counselor, who informed him that he might have post traumatic stress disorder from his chaotic past. I wanted to be empathetic, but my patience was growing thin as the tension in our home grew thicker.

I decided to attend college part time and got a job at the on-campus daycare. My son went to work with me. The busy routine was a welcome change of pace and a nice escape from the chaos in my home. Raul had refused to keep going to counseling, and our marriage was hanging on by a thread. As my belly swelled, reminding me of new life inside of me, it seemed my marriage was dying a slow death.

One night, I woke up to find Raul wasn't in the bed with me. I went downstairs and was enraged to find him watching another porn video. The bubble of anger I'd been trying to suppress finally burst, and I punched the living room window as hard as I could. The window shattered, blood spattered everywhere and my hand instantly throbbed. I yanked it back, shocked that I'd mustered enough force to break through the glass.

"What the h*** are you doing?" Raul screamed, his eyes ablaze as he glared at me. "Are you crazy?" He stormed out the front door and went to sit in his car.

I stood there, angry and horrified, writhing in pain as I watched the blood drip onto the floor. After what felt like forever, Raul finally marched back into the house and grudgingly drove me to the emergency room. I wanted to hurl every hurtful word imaginable at him while we drove, but I was in so much pain I could hardly speak. When we arrived at the hospital, the doctors stitched me up and sent me home.

I knew we'd reached a new low. We could not go on this way. We were toxic for one another. Yet I was due with a new baby soon, and I was still determined to make things work. We tried counseling, but Raul seemed checked out. I had never imagined my marriage being like this, and it struck me as ironic that I could share a bed with someone and yet feel lonelier than I ever had in my life.

My second son was born in 1999, and I was overjoyed. Perhaps Raul would finally change his ways now that he had another child. But to my chagrin, he returned to his old behavior and began going out late at night again. At my wit's end, I decided to hire a private investigator. I had made up my mind that if another woman was involved, I would not stay with Raul. Infidelity would be the final straw.

The private investigator followed Raul one night and came back to report the bad news to me. "I found your husband meeting a lady in the park," the investigator informed me. "They were walking a dog, and he wound up going home with her."

I took short, ragged breaths, trying to absorb the devastating information. "Thank you. That's all I need to know," I muttered.

I confronted Raul and told him I'd hired a private investigator. "He has footage of you with another woman, so don't try to deny it," I told him angrily. "I'm done. I want a divorce."

To my surprise, Raul didn't deny it or put up a fight. I filed for divorce and obtained full custody of our boys. He disappeared from our lives for a while, and I tried my best to resume life as a single parent. When he eventually called wanting to see the boys every other weekend, I was hesitant. I didn't trust his behavior or his judgment, so to protect my children and to be extra cautious before agreeing to his request, I was adamant that he get drug tested before spending time with our young sons.

With the divorce finalized, my self-esteem plummeted to a new low. I had seen my brother, my husband and my father all fall into the grips of pornography, lured by the beautiful women of their fantasies. I knew I would never measure up to those women, but perhaps if I just tried a little harder to improve my looks, men would see me in a new light.

Suddenly, food became the enemy. A plate of pasta was now evil, and desserts taunted me from the cupboard shelves. I became determined to eat as little as possible, knowing full well that the women of glossy magazine pages and television were all ultra-thin. I hopped on the treadmill each day, sometimes exercising so much that I nearly dropped to the ground from exhaustion. The pounds slowly melted off, and my clothes grew baggier each week. But I still wasn't satisfied.

When I glanced in the mirror, I hated the girl staring back at me. Disgusted with my looks, I decided to cover all the mirrors in my house to avoid catching my reflection. In the morning, I peeked through a tiny slit in the paper over the bathroom mirror to apply my makeup. I also stuck a photo of a starving African person on my refrigerator as "inspiration." My weight continued to drop, but I still loathed the way I looked.

One day, after spending an hour and a half on the treadmill on a near-empty stomach, I fell to the floor sobbing. My life was falling apart, and I didn't have a clue how to fix it. I was angry with my ex-husband for the way his behavior tormented me over the years, but I was even angrier with myself. I hated the way I looked on the outside, but I hated the insecurity that plagued me as well. Life felt hopeless and empty.

I slipped off my shoes and glanced down at my feet; big blisters had formed on the bottom of them. *Ugly, ugly feet,* I thought to myself, shaking my head. Exhausted, I closed my eyes for just a few moments. As I did, I saw water being poured over my feet and a pair of masculine hands washing them. Immediately, I knew just who those hands belonged to — Jesus. There's a story in the Bible about Jesus washing the feet of his friends. Usually, servants had the job of washing men's dirty feet at the end of the day. The job was considered the lowest of the low. But Jesus took the time to wash his friends' feet. It was an act of humility and love. Now, in the midst of my exhaustion and desperation, Jesus was washing my feet, covering my brokenness with his gentle love.

I opened my eyes, unsure if I'd fallen asleep or passed out. Nevertheless, I knew what I'd seen was real. I had had a vision of Jesus washing my feet, and it had brought great comfort to me in my despair. I sensed his presence in the room as I stood up and glanced out the kitchen window. Outside, the sky looked bluer than it had before, and everything around me seemed brighter. The great heaviness that had shrouded me for so long seemed to lift at that moment, and I thanked God for what he had shown me. Even when I felt too ashamed to approach him, he had reminded me that he was still near. He had not forgotten me.

"You should get out there and date again," my friends from church suggested. "We know a guy we'd like to set you up with."

I agreed to go on the date, but halfway through it, I realized I was wasting my time. When I went to the bathroom that evening, I glanced in the mirror and grimaced. *Look how fat you are,* I told myself angrily, inspecting my reflection. *No one's going to like you the way you are.*

Suddenly, an idea came to me. *Maybe I could throw up. Just this once. I'll rid myself of the meal I just ate, and the calories will disappear.*

I forced myself to throw up in the toilet, surprised at how easy it was. Instantly, relief flooded me. I'd been spending hours on the treadmill, sweaty and exhausted, when I could have just chosen this option instead! Why hadn't I thought of it sooner?

My new plan seemed brilliant. I could eat anything I wanted and not gain weight! I began eating full meals again, piling my plate high with food and binging on snacks in between. The minute I finished my meal, I retreated to the bathroom, where I promptly threw up and watched the food disappear down the toilet. The rest of my world had spun out of control, but this was one thing I *could* control. Deep down, however, guilt ate away at me. I decided I'd keep my little secret to myself. No one would have to know what I did behind closed doors.

As the months passed, I soon realized I could not keep supporting myself on my own. I moved back in with my parents and obtained government assistance to help pay the bills. I continued attending college and working as a part-time daycare provider at a church. The one-hour commute each way took a toll on me. I binged and purged several times a day, all the while hiding my secret from the world. My clothes became baggier, my body shook constantly and my hair began to fall out in chunks. I hated the person I had become, but I didn't know how to escape the prison I'd created for myself.

Determined to get back out on my own, I found a two-bedroom basement apartment I could afford, unfortunately in one of the roughest neighborhoods in town. The day I moved in, I saw a large, greasy-haired guy sitting on the front porch of the complex, smoking a cigarette.

"Hello," I squeaked, a bit frightened by his intimidating appearance.

"Watch out for the worms," he said with a strange smile.

Okay, freaky dude, whatever, I thought as I slipped past him. But as I headed through the front door, I walked right into a tangle of silk strings made from worms hanging from the roof above. I shuddered. What had I gotten myself into?

As I lay in bed at night, listening to the blaring horns, gunshots and shouts outside my dingy little place, I realized I'd reached a new low. Bulimia now ruled my life. My days revolved around eating and throwing up. I hated that I kept such a dark secret from everyone I loved. I grew angry with God. I had tried being a good wife and a good person, yet my husband had failed me, along with every other man I knew.

I tried it your way, God, but it didn't work out very well, so I'm going to do what I want, I told him defiantly.

I'll do whatever it takes to be beautiful so that I can live up to the standards of these men.

As my life continued to unravel, strange things began to occur at home. One day, when I stepped into the bathroom, the glass vase on the toilet shattered into pieces before my eyes. I shuddered as I swept up the pieces and threw them in the trash. The vase had been a wedding gift. Though I'd gotten rid of most of the items from my marriage, I'd held on to this one piece. The fact that it had shattered on its own was odd, but things were about to get even stranger.

During the following week, several more unexplainable things happened. The mini-blinds suddenly popped off my window, the TV turned on several times in the middle of the night and the rear windshield of my car broke into splintery pieces out of the blue. *What is going on around here?* I wondered, suddenly terrified. It was as if a dangerous presence had chosen to inhabit my home and haunt me. Had I done something to invite such darkness in?

I decided to seek counseling, but I didn't find it helpful. Though I switched counselors several times, each session felt just the same as the last. I shared about my struggles with bulimia, but no one offered any real solutions. I left feeling defeated and misunderstood. My weight continued to plummet, falling below 100 pounds. My clothes hung off my 5-foot, 5-inch frame, but I still wasn't satisfied with my looks. To boost my self-esteem, I decided to start going to nightclubs. I carefully applied my makeup, combed my hair and slipped on my sexiest outfit. The dance floor was packed as I walked into the dark nightclub one evening. Loud hip-hop music blared, and slick-haired guys sidled up to girls to offer them a drink and a dance. As I stepped forward, I watched several guys' heads turn.

This is it, I told myself, slightly smug. *You could have any guy in here you want, Angel.* My heart thumped along with the music as I mulled the realization over in my mind. I was becoming the very thing I hated — a sexual object to men. It was terrifying and satisfying at the same time.

I continued going to the clubs and dancing with guys. I wanted someone to take me home, yet it never happened. However, one night, I met a guy named Luke. He seemed different than everyone else, and as he pulled me aside to talk, I learned that he was an artist. Like me, he was also divorced.

"So why did your marriage end? What happened?" I pressed, the drinks making me bold.

Luke shrugged. "I had a porn addiction. She couldn't handle it anymore."

"Oh." Immediately, my heart sank. *Just another guy addicted to porn. They're all the same.* Yet something intrigued me about Luke; he seemed to have real depth. We continued talking, and before long, we began dating.

One day, Luke told me his work was going to be featured in an art show at a local museum. "You gotta come check it out," he told me.

Luke's work was, in fact, a collage made from porn magazines. He had taken strips of women's skin and glued them together in a strangely beautiful way. I stared at the collage, impressed yet disturbed. Once again, here were women's bodies on display. I didn't quite know how to respond.

I continued taking classes at the college. One day, a professor invited our class upstairs to watch a porn video a student had made. He said it was considered an art form. I was taken aback by his suggestion. It seemed sex was everywhere I turned. My stomach lurched as I headed downstairs and opted out of the activity.

As I stepped out the doors, I saw a guy from my class on the phone.

"They want us to watch this porn video, but I'm not gonna do it, honey," he said.

I sucked in my breath as I continued to eavesdrop. *He must be talking to his wife,* I realized. *Wow! At least there's one man out there with some integrity left!* I walked away with a sliver of hope in my heart. Perhaps there really were a few good guys left out there after all. But it didn't matter. No decent guy would ever want me. What could I possibly have to offer them?

I broke up with Luke a couple months later. Life became a monotonous struggle. Often, I took food home from work because I could not afford to go to the store. I continued the vicious cycle of binging and purging, and I hated myself for it. Raul remained minimally involved in the boys' lives and did not offer me financial support. I wondered if I would ever find the means to escape my desperate, lonely situation.

One night, after stuffing myself with a few cheap gas station pastries, I went into the bathroom to purge. As I tried to throw up, the pastry got caught in my throat, and I started to choke. My eyes watered as my throat constricted, and panic seized me. *I cannot breathe. I am going to die right here on this bathroom floor, choking on the very thing that's been killing me emotionally,* I realized in horror.

At last, I gasped for air, and I was able to breathe again. But as I flushed the toilet, and the filthy water rose until it spilled over the edge, tears spilled down my cheeks as I realized I'd sunk to a whole new low. I was literally at my end.

"God, please heal me or take me out of this world!" I cried desperately. "I cannot do this anymore!" My mind flashed to the time I'd taken my father's gun out into the woods; I'd never felt so alone. I hadn't pulled the trigger that day, but I wondered what it might be like if that gun was in my hands now. I was ready to end it all if my life did not soon turn around.

I pulled myself together that night, got my boys ready the next morning and headed off to work. Before I left, I took one last glance in the mirror and cringed at what I saw. I still wasn't satisfied with my looks, and I didn't like the girl who stared back at me. It struck me as ironic that while I hid behind baggy clothes, I was also pleading with the world to be seen. I harbored a dark secret I could not share with those closest to me, yet I wished that just once someone would ask me about my heart. I wished someone would ask me if I was okay, so I could tell him that I wasn't at all.

A few weeks later, I met a guy named Bruce at church where I worked as a caregiver. He was handsome and pleasant, and I enjoyed our brief conversations. After talking several times, I worked up the courage to ask him if he wanted my phone number.

Bruce smiled kindly and paused for a moment. "I'll pray about it," he replied politely.

I was stunned. I had never met a guy who had such boundaries. Instead of feeling disappointed, I gained respect for my new friend. Bruce talked often about his relationship with God, and I could tell it was genuine. He was not like the guys at the clubs who ogled every girl who walked in; he was a true gentleman. I remained content and believed that if Bruce wanted to pursue things with me, he would make the next move.

Bruce finally agreed to let me make dinner for him. I was excited to prepare one of my favorite meals. Though our conversation flowed easily, panic crept into the back of my mind. I was accustomed to throwing up after every meal. I'd have to get rid of Bruce right after dinner so I could run to the bathroom and purge. But what if he found out? What would he think of me then?

Bruce came over for dinner several times, and each time after we ate, I quietly slipped out to the bathroom. One evening, however, he announced he wasn't leaving right away. "I'm going to stay for a while, if you don't mind," he said, smiling.

Again, panic rose in my chest, and my heart began to race. I had to get to that bathroom and throw up! But to my shock, Bruce walked over to the bathroom and blocked the door. I began to cry, tears spilling down my cheeks as I realized he knew my terrible secret.

"It's okay, Angel," he said softly. "I'm not going anywhere. You're going to be okay." He bowed his head and began to pray, asking God to be with me in this moment and give me comfort. He did not taunt me or make me feel bad about myself, but instead, in true gentlemanly fashion, he showed up for me at my darkest hour. Instead of humiliating me, he simply loved me as I was.

No one has ever showed up for me like this, I thought to myself, stunned.

"We're going to get through this, Angel," Bruce encouraged me before he left. "I'm here for you."

Each night he came over for dinner, I pushed my food around my plate and began to cry. The thought of actually digesting it and letting it stay in my body seemed crazy. Food was supposed to be the enemy, not something I enjoyed. But each time I glanced up at Bruce's reassuring face, I felt a newfound ease. Despite my shameful disorder, he remained patient and kind. What had I done to deserve a man this good in my life?

I continued to throw up at work, but when I was with Bruce, I tried to keep the food down. My mouth and throat were sore from resurfacing stomach acid, my hands were a ruddy pink and my hair continued to fall out. I knew I was destroying my body, but I wasn't sure I'd ever be able to maintain a sense of normalcy again.

One day, as I hovered over schoolwork at the kitchen table, I saw a little girl sitting next to me. She looked about 6 years old and was holding a blanket. I opened my mouth and let out a scream. Just as I began to panic, she quickly disappeared. My heart thudded in my chest as I stared at the space she had been just moments ago. Had I imagined her? Was my mind playing tricks on me?

"What is it?" Bruce asked, flying into the room.

I could hardly explain what I'd seen. Was that little girl me all those years ago?

I decided to see a new counselor. As I pulled up at her office, I panicked and considered driving away. But suddenly I stopped in my tracks. Before me, I had another vision that seemed both real and unreal. I saw myself, running as fast as I could from something terrifying. My heart thudded in my ears. I ducked around a corner to hide and saw a strange chaotic vortex-spinning object pass by me. Instantly, I realized my back was up against something, and when I looked up, it was the throne of God. When I glanced back down, I was clad in chainmail armor.

The vision both shook me up and excited me. My eyes had been open the entire time. Was it real? Was it from God? Though I cannot fully explain it, I believe God was telling me that I was a warrior.

I was fighting a battle, but I was not fighting it alone.

The new counselor I began seeing educated me on nutrition in an eye-opening way. "Your body needs a certain amount of calories each day to maintain brain and kidney function," she explained. "Without those calories, your vital organs will start to shut down."

Her words were meant to shake me up, but instead I thought to myself, *Okay, I'll just eat the minimum amount of calories each day to keep my body from shutting down.* I still could not look at food as my friend.

Despite my struggle, I slowly opened my heart to Bruce. I had never met such a kind, wonderful man who loved me unconditionally. I often tested him, lashing out to see how he reacted. Every other guy in my life had let me down in one way or another. Was Bruce too good to be true? Would he leave me if I pushed the limits too far? And did he really want to be with me — a struggling single mother of two boys?

Though not always perfect, Bruce remained by my side, never once shaming me but instead loving me through my pain. My ex-husband was hardly around anymore, and I knew my young boys needed a father-figure in their life. Bruce would make a wonderful husband, I was sure of that. One thing was certain — I was falling in love with this man.

As Bruce and I continued dating, Raul began to get his life back together again. He called, wanting to see the boys more frequently. Bruce was hesitant to share the boys with him, as he had really bonded with them.

"I don't know how this is all going to work," Bruce confessed to me.

"You're amazing with the boys," I reminded him. "I know this isn't easy, but we're all going to figure this out."

Bruce invited me back east for his brother's wedding, and I agreed to go. While visiting his family, I noticed he was suddenly acting strange. We stopped at a grocery store, and when I tried to follow him down the aisle, he darted away. I saw a group of cute girls nearby and assumed he was going off to flirt with them, and my cheeks flamed. What was going on?

That night, we drove out to a nearby lake. The stars shone bright as the water below shimmered in the moonlight, and I snuggled close to Bruce, relishing the romantic setting. Suddenly, Bruce turned to me and uttered the words I had longed to hear him say since we first met.

"Angel, I love you," he whispered, his eyes searching mine. "Will you marry me?"

"Yes!" I cried, overwhelmed with joy. Bruce had once told me he would not tell a girl he loved her unless he was ready to propose. Though he had shown his love in a million ways since we began dating, he had saved these sacred, beautiful words until this perfect moment.

He presented me with a rose, which he confessed he'd been trying to buy in the store without me knowing. I laughed, realizing I'd thought he was going off to flirt with those girls. How wrong I had been — Bruce only had eyes for me! Despite all my struggles, Bruce found me beautiful and lovable, and he truly cherished me. I could hardly comprehend such a love, but I was sure that if there was really such a thing as a modern knight in shining armor, Bruce was definitely mine.

Bruce and I married in 2002, six months after he proposed. We had a small family-only ceremony that included a special foot-washing ceremony. The ritual was especially meaningful to me after the vision I'd had of Jesus washing my blistered feet. Through Bruce, I had seen Jesus' love in human form. I had never known such compassion and love, and I could hardly wait to start my life with him.

Over the next year, I continued to work through my struggles. Bruce remained patient with me as I fought my disease. Slowly, I began to see food as fuel for my body instead of something that would make me fat. And slowly, I began to love myself again. I no longer cringed when I looked in the mirror, but instead I started to see myself as Bruce did, and as Jesus did, too. I was God's beloved daughter, not a worthless, ugly girl. God loved me with all my scars, wounds and brokenness, and so did Bruce.

As a child, I had been taught that Jesus was my best friend. When I was 8 years old, I had walked forward in my little cowboy boots at church, excited to invite him into my heart. The gospel message of the Bible had been so simple to me then. God had sent his son, Jesus, to earth to die on the cross for the wrong things we'd done. He knew we would all mess up throughout our lives, but because he loved us so much, he had sacrificed his only son so that we could spend eternity in heaven with him if we invited him in. As I'd grown older, I'd learned how to have a real relationship with Jesus. I could come to him with my deepest desires, hurts and joys, and he would listen to me. He loved me, and I loved him.

But since I had fallen into the depths of my sickness, I no longer felt I could share my heart with Jesus. Surely, he must be mad at me. Surely, he must be as disgusted with me as I was with myself. How could he love me when I was hiding such a terrible secret from the world? I was ashamed and filled with guilt.

Now, as I stepped free of the chains that had entangled me for so long, I realized that my story was really no different than anyone else's. From the man struggling with pornography to the girl battling bulimia, we were all searching for the same thing: love. There was an emptiness inside us all that could only be filled with Jesus, and until we fully let him capture our hearts, ask him to cleanse us and learn to rest in his love, we would never be satisfied. I was finally able to forgive the men who had hurt me because I saw their humanity, and in the process, I was able to forgive myself.

I threw out all my beauty magazines, no longer interested in comparing myself to the airbrushed models between the pages. I also decided to stop watching TV so I wasn't flooded with images of "perfect" people. These changes felt freeing, and I knew I was finally on the road to healing.

But my journey was not over. I continued to push and test Bruce to see if his love for me was real. Could I really trust him, or would he disappoint me?

One day, I came home to find Bruce watching a country music video. A partially clothed couple was having sex on the screen, and my heart skipped a beat. "What are you watching?" I screamed, freaking out.

"Calm down. It's just a Garth Brooks video," Bruce replied coolly.

I tried to calm down, but I was suddenly irate. The image on the screen had triggered an old wound deep inside and provoked an irrational reaction. When I was able to compose myself, I turned to God and prayed, asking him to replace my fears with his truth. I felt his peace wash over me, and I thanked him for comforting me.

In 2005, we moved an hour away, and I gave birth to my third child. As our little boy entered the world, Bruce sat nearby, cheering from the sidelines like a supportive coach. It was a beautiful moment for us all.

We began attending Northgate Alaska, and I was impressed with the transparency among the church members. All of them, I learned, had something difficult in their life, yet the atmosphere allowed for people to share openly and put their hearts on the line. I thought about the lonely years I'd spent hiding my eating disorder from the world, feeling too ashamed to bare my soul. It was refreshing to know that my new friends embraced me and my family just as we were, imperfections and all.

In 2007, I graduated college with a Bachelor's degree, and the following year, I began graduate work. As a single mother living in a rough neighborhood on government assistance, I often wondered if I would actually accomplish my goal and graduate college. Yet God had been so faithful, providing not just my basic needs, but giving me more than my heart could ever have desired.

Bruce and I bought a beautiful home and began pursuing our dreams to start our own business. In 2010, I gave birth to a fourth child, a little girl. We were elated to complete our family. Not long after she was born, Bruce told me he and Raul were going to take our older two boys to see the new inspirational movie, *Courageous*. Raul, by then remarried, had become a more active part of the boys' lives. God had truly healed our relationship, and I loved his wife as well. I was grateful that we had made such big strides since those tumultuous days years ago. Since understanding grace — the wonderful idea that God loves me, even though I've done nothing to deserve it — I was able to genuinely extend it to others, even those who had once hurt me deeply.

Bruce and the boys returned from the movie, excited to share the message they'd learned. "The movie was a good reminder that husbands and fathers need to step up to the plate and be the godly men the world needs them to be," he told me. "I really hope I can be that man for you, Angel."

As Bruce pulled me into his arms, I thanked God once again for this beautiful gift. Our relationship had not been perfect, but I never once doubted that he was the man for me. I was thrilled that he wanted to be courageous, to fight for my honor and do what was right before God. I only hoped my boys would grow up to be half as strong as him.

ॐॐॐ

I stood before the bathroom mirror, splashing water on my face as I prepared for the day. I'd seen my face a thousand times, but the girl staring back at me was not the same girl of my past. Once upon a time, I'd covered my mirrors so I would not have to see the reflection I loathed. I'd been a prisoner of my own worst nightmare, a gaunt, thin girl hiding a secret from the world. I'd been so sure God did not love me — surely, he must be disgusted with me, too.

Today, 10 years after marrying Bruce, that girl smiles back at me. There is color in her cheeks, but more importantly, there is life again inside her heart.

As I dab on my makeup and take one last glance in the mirror before walking away, I thank God for all he's done in my life. Just as my favorite Bible verse, Psalm 40:2 (NIV) reads, "He lifted me out of the slimy pit, out of the mud and mire. He set my feet on a rock and gave me a firm place to stand." I'd once sat in the mud and mire in my own bathroom, wondering how I'd ever escape from my slimy pit. But God pulled me right out of that pit, sending Bruce into my life to show me just how much Jesus loves me.

I had never been alone, and I never would be, because the Jesus I'd invited into my heart as a child was the same Jesus who'd washed my blistered feet and walked with me through my pain. I am beautiful in his eyes, and that is all I need to know.

HIGHER

The Story of Brian Kincaid
Written by Joy Steiner Moore

Snow swirled around me as I stumbled blindly up the mountainside. The terrain was rugged, and the 150-mile-per-hour winds certainly weren't helping my climb. I zipped up my windbreaker, but the icy Alaskan cold cut right through it. The chill was nearly paralyzing.

Can't stop, I thought to myself, forcing my body forward against the elements.

Wet snow mixed with ice pellets were hitting my face, stinging my skin, and the roar of the wind filled my ears like the sound of a passing train.

I had remembered seeing an ice cave at the top of Sharatin Mountain, and now, with my team's camp and equipment ripped away by winds in the middle of the night, this shelter, if I could find it, was the only thing that could save my life. I wasn't dressed for this kind of weather. My team members were somewhere below. They had been able to put their survival suits on while I made the distress call on the satellite phone. But in the chaos of the storm, we had become separated, and now it was each man for himself. So I trudged on.

In all my years of "pushing limits," I had never been *this* afraid — this certain that I was facing the end.

I must be near the top by now. The ground had leveled somewhat, but even with my flashlight, I couldn't see more than five feet in front of me — maybe less than that. There was just too much snow. Looking for the entrance to the cave would be like searching for a needle in a haystack. And with the dropping temperature, I knew time was running out.

My body trembled violently as another gust of icy wind threatened to knock me over.

"God, if you don't show up right now, I'm a dead man!" I screamed into the wind.

Suddenly, out of nowhere, a tunnel seemed to form in the snow in front of me. The storm continued to rage around it, but it was like a definite path had been cleared just for me. Shocked, I aimed the beam of my flashlight through the tunnel, and there, at the very end, was the opening I was searching for — the entrance to the ice cave.

Within a matter of seconds, I was safe inside. I glanced over my shoulder at the blizzard I had just narrowly escaped.

The tunnel was gone.

෨෨෨

From the very beginning, my mom told me, she always knew there was a battle for my life. I developed a scary bout of pneumonia as a newborn. My lungs collapsed several times, and I almost didn't make it.

As a toddler, I had a serious tricycle wreck, leaving

deep scars on my forehead. And that was just the start of it.

I grew up in rural Palmer, Alaska, at the end of a long dirt road. Our small one-story house was surrounded by farming fields and woods, and my five older siblings and I had plenty of room to roam. It was the 1960s and '70s, which was the height of Evel Knievel's career, and I became obsessed with developing daredevil antics of my own. I was a bit of a loner, so it was nothing for me to head out by myself in the morning and spend the whole day building jumps and creating stunts in the wild. My parents didn't worry. They'd let me do my thing and then call me home at night in time for dinner. In the evenings, I rebuilt motorcycles in the small bedroom I shared with my two brothers. I lived on the thrill of adventure and thrived on the warm rush of adrenaline coursing through my veins.

My biggest obstacle, however, was my speech. I stuttered. I was the brunt of jokes at school and was embarrassed among my classmates. I was socially awkward and never felt like I fit in with anyone. Even when I was soaring through the air with the rush of backcountry extreme sports, I knew deep down that stuttering was something I couldn't control and couldn't overcome. So I kept pushing myself toward higher and higher stunts. These were the things I *could* overcome — that made me feel good inside. I wanted more and more. The high I got off of it was addicting. But it still wasn't enough.

My parents had enrolled me in speech therapy for six years, and I finally came into my own around sixth grade. Speaking better gave me a bit more confidence in myself — enough to invite some classmates over to go camping on my 12th birthday.

We pitched our tents in the raw wilderness behind my house, and I gathered supplies for a raging campfire. But there was something else that I thought might be fun, too. While my parents were preoccupied, I snuck into the pantry and stole a couple of bottles of my dad's homemade wine, hiding them safely inside my backpack.

"Do you guys want a drink?" I asked my friends later as we were gathered around the fire, exchanging stories and enjoying the crisp, cool summer night.

"Sure," one replied. "What do you have?"

I leaned over and reached into my backpack.

"This," I said, pulling out one of the bottles with a sheepish grin.

"Awesome!"

"Oh, yeah!"

I'd never had alcohol before, and I didn't know whether they had or not. But in keeping with my daredevil spirit, I was hell bent on trying it.

The next morning we were all sick as dogs, but I had no regrets. I had impressed my friends and successfully navigated another risky experience. And my parents never knew.

దావాదా

I was literally the very definition of adrenaline junkie. Before I was 25, I owned my own rear-engine rail racecar and drag-racing team. I had built the car from the ground up, and I called it "The Adrenaline Factory." We traveled the Alaska racing circuit for about a year. I was fearless, of course, so I was also very good at it, often placing highly in races and then winning the coveted Rookie of the Year award.

On one particular race day in Fairbanks, I was in my motor home getting ready for the big event. I had just showered and dressed, and my white flame suit and helmet were laid out across my bed. I stood at the mirror and ran a comb through my hair.

I need a drink.

I had about 15 minutes until I needed to be ready, I figured, so I headed for the tiny kitchenette. Drinking had become a sporadic pleasure for me over the years. I didn't need alcohol all the time, but when I indulged, I did it big time.

Picking out a whisky glass, I set it on the counter. The bottle clinked against the glass as I poured. When I sat down at the table, it wasn't just for the whisky, however. I pulled out my stashes of cocaine and marijuana, too. I had just snorted a line of coke when, without warning, a fellow racer walked in.

"Brian, are you ready, dude?"

It didn't take him long to figure out what was going on. He stood in the doorway of the motor home, his mouth gaping in shock. I stared back, daring him to say anything to the other guys. I was good at what I did out there. It didn't make a difference what I did in here.

"What is *wrong* with you?" His eyes were intense, and the disgust and bewilderment were evident on his face. He turned on his heel, closing the motor home door tightly behind him on his way out.

Though I wouldn't admit it, the problem was that it was never enough. It wasn't enough to race hundreds of miles an hour in a dragster. I needed alcohol and drugs on top of it. My needs were insatiable.

After a year of racing, I was eager for the next rush, so I was on to aerobatics, then snowmobiling, among many other endeavors.

It was always something new, but it was never, ever enough.

ళళళ

In addition to my continued participation in extreme sports, I landed my dream job in communications and fiber optics. I traveled the world and lived an exciting life building infrastructure for data, cell phones and Internet. For a daredevil like me, the job was perfect. Using helicopters and airplanes was just another day's work. Remote locations and mountaintops were my office. Dynamite was my pen and paper. I rented beautiful houses on my company's dime and had access to large amounts of funds on my company credit card. My brand-new Corvette was my pride and joy.

My coworkers' motto was the same as mine: work hard, drink hard. The alcoholism and drug use had become a problem, but because I was good at my job, my supervisors chose to overlook it.

In the meantime, though I was a bachelor in every sense of the word, I was beginning to feel the need for companionship. I was 32 years old when I met Alisa, a spunky restaurant cook, when I ordered the Cajun chicken at the restaurant where she worked. After a heated disagreement over the menu, I knew I kind of liked her, so I invited her to come over and ride one of my snow machines. And when she tucked her blond ponytail into her knit winter hat and clocked 100 miles per hour, I knew I wanted to ask her on a real date.

Alisa was like no girl I had ever met. She was a strong long-distance runner who competed in mountain marathons. Watching her passion for running was like watching my passion for extreme sports. We were married a year later on Valentine's Day.

I had promised Alisa her dream home: a log house on a big property in the mountains with a stream running by it. So, a few years into our marriage, we set out to make that dream come true. We found the picture-perfect property near Hatcher Pass, just up the mountain from Palmer, and we began construction on it. But everything was about to change.

❧❧❧

"I need you to sign right here for me," the delivery man said, handing me his clipboard and a pen.

I glanced at the bundled lumber stacked neatly in the yard. I did a quick count and double-checked the paperwork.

"Looks good to me," I agreed, signing the delivery receipt.

"A storm's blowing in. Are you planning on doing much more work today?"

I lifted my eyes to the western range, where dark, ominous clouds were moving quickly toward us.

"Nah. Just need to make sure everything's watertight." I smiled. "Thanks for the delivery."

"Sure thing."

The delivery man swung into his truck and carefully maneuvered it down the long driveway. As I turned toward the house, I felt the first raindrops. I hustled across the yard.

"Alisa! A storm's coming!"

The wind had already picked up, too.

I climbed the ladder to the unfinished roof and began fastening the tarp as quickly as I could. The heavens opened, and I found myself wrestling with a knot in the rope amidst a steady downpour. In a split moment of unsteadiness, my feet suddenly slipped, and I lost my balance. I felt myself sliding, and my arms flailed wildly, trying to grab anything up there that might stop my fall. But it was all happening too fast. My body tumbled off the roof, sailed through the air and landed on an uneven pile of construction debris and rough concrete slabs down below.

Instant pain seared through my pelvis, like nothing I had ever felt before in my life. I cried out in agony. I didn't think I could stand it. The pain was absolutely overwhelming.

"Brian!" Alisa ran toward me, scrambling over the concrete to my side.

"No. Don't touch me," I growled.

It was raining hard now, and we were getting soaked.

"Where are you hurt?" Alisa grabbed my hand, her hair hanging around her face in wet ringlets. I winced.

"Don't touch me!" I barked. "It's my leg. Call the paramedics. Please."

"Okay. Take deep breaths," she ordered.

I just closed my eyes, lifted my face to the falling rain and waited.

≈≈≈

At the hospital in Wasilla, I learned the horrible truth: My pelvis was shattered.

"Your husband will never walk again," the doctor told Alisa.

I was crushed and understandably so. I, who had climbed mountains, driven race cars, jumped ATVs, flown aerobatics and competed in 500-mile snowmobile races, would never walk again? It wasn't possible. I had lived large. I had been extremely confident in my physicality.

And I had lost the ability to walk by falling off a stupid roof?

This can't be happening. I won't let it happen.

I was sent to a specialist in Anchorage, where they eventually performed hip surgery, using 28 screws to put me back together. I went through months of physical therapy, during which I could not work. My company was very supportive and continued to pay my salary while I began the slow, painful process of recovery.

But in the meantime, I had been taking large doses of Oxycodone to control the pain, and I had become dependent on the drug to get me from hour to hour. When I combined that with severe depression and half a bottle of whisky a day, I was a strung-out mess. I was irrational and extremely difficult to live with.

Alisa and I had three small children at the time, and she couldn't stand to see me going downhill like that. Even more so, based on her childhood experiences with her own father, she didn't want our boys to see me that way. So she packed up what they needed, kissed me goodbye and went to go stay with her mother, leaving me alone in our beautiful home — now complete, but no longer seeming quite so dreamy.

I was such a mess. I felt like a broken man — so very far from the confident daredevil I had been. The drugs and alcohol had stolen my life from me. It wasn't just the fall off the roof, I realized. It wasn't just the broken pelvis. It was the choices I had made my entire life in trying to fill the hole in my heart — in trying to satisfy the need for having/being/living *enough*. I had never been content. I had always needed more.

But now I didn't want to live. I just wanted *out*. I planned to drink and drug myself into nothingness.

I had nearly hit rock bottom when my mother arrived to see what she could do. She let herself in and began searching for me throughout the house.

"Brian? Hello?"

Her voice sounded a million miles away from the bedroom where I lay, but it was comforting, nonetheless. I learned later that, since I hadn't been answering the phone, she had driven up to the house thinking it very well might be a body recovery. She didn't know how close it was to being just that.

༄༄༄

With Alisa's and my mom's help, I landed in Teen Challenge, a treatment center and rehabilitation program for substance abuse. They made me go cold turkey off of everything I had been on — Oxycodone, alcohol, cocaine, you name it. They placed me in a large room with a dozen other patients and took away all means of contacting my family or friends.

I lay in bed awake for seven solid days, utterly miserable and unable to sleep a wink. My mind felt chaotic. A tumultuous war raged within me.

But then, out of nowhere, the strangest thing happened. Though I lay in a bed in the detoxing unit at

Teen Challenge, I clearly saw myself lying in a beautiful green meadow, my wife and children sitting in the grass beside me. The image was so real to me. I felt like I could reach out and touch it. A gentle stream flowed quietly nearby, and in a tree above us, Jesus sat casually, watching over us and smiling.

Jesus?

I had been raised in church and had attended a little bit of church as an adult, so I was somewhat familiar with the idea of God sending his son, Jesus, to earth to save us from the angst and confusion we had brought upon ourselves. But I had never experienced his *peace* like this before.

All of the uncertainty and disorder suddenly melted away. My need for an adrenaline rush was stilled. The entire scene brought unexplainable calmness to my spirit and replaced the chaos with tranquility.

Beautiful words I had learned long ago in Sunday school filled my mind:

> "The LORD is my shepherd, I shall not want.
> He makes me lie down in green pastures;
> He leads me beside quiet waters.
> He restores my soul …" (Psalm 23:1-3 ESV).

It seemed so strange, but that was exactly what I felt like he was doing. He was *restoring my soul*. Down to the green pastures and quiet water, he had brought these ancient words to life in a vision just for me to see.

For the first time since I could remember, I felt complete.

"I shall not want." Being with him is enough.

In the midst of the physical and mental pain, in the midst of my confusion, when I had absolutely nothing left to offer myself or anyone else, the son of God was entering the scene and saying, "Find your peace in me." No gimmicks. No stunts. No payment required. He was just promising to be enough.

He's enough.

I clung to the vision of the meadow for the next four days, and my soul finally found the rest and contentment I had been searching for my entire life.

❧❧❧

I stayed at Teen Challenge for a full month. By this time I had been unable to work for an entire year, but the good news was that in addition to getting through my addictions, my ability to walk had been improving greatly, defying the first doctor's prediction. I moved back home, and Alisa and the kids moved back in, too. I went back to work and, inspired by my peaceful vision in rehab, decided to also start going to church again.

It wasn't a piece of cake. After all, I had been abusing alcohol for years. In fact, I found multiple excuses to slip into my old ways and go on drinking binges in the years that followed, and I had several serious setbacks. On a business trip to Kodiak, a hotel bartender watched as I drank myself into near oblivion. Eventually, on the fourth day, she became concerned and called the paramedics. They broke into my hotel room and discovered my near-lifeless body. My eyes and skin were yellow, and my liver was shutting down. After a hospital stay, I became a regular at Alcoholics Anonymous meetings, sometimes attending three a day. I had a good support system and a list of phone numbers to call should I feel any urge whatsoever.

I became convinced that I had two choices: sobering up or certain death. If I wanted to live long enough to see my sons grow up, I knew that I had to make radical changes in my life. I couldn't keep repeating the pattern of destruction.

Deep down, I held on to the vision that God had given me. I wanted that peace in my heart — not just sometimes, but *all* the time. I finally emptied myself *of myself* enough that there was finally room for Jesus to come in and do his thing full-time.

I read these words of Jesus in my Bible:

> "Peace I leave with you; my peace I give you.
> I do not give to you as the world gives.
> Do not let your hearts be troubled
> and do not be afraid" (John 14:27 NIV).

What I had been seeking with chemicals, I filled with spirituality — with a relationship with the very one who had created me, who knew my every need.

HIGHER

ぞぞぞ

A few years later, I headed up a four-man team to complete a company project on Sharatin Mountain on Kodiak Island. We were dropped off by a helicopter and began working right away. But what began as a perfect, sunny day for our expedition quickly turned into a nightmare around 1:30 a.m. A winter storm moved in within a matter of minutes, and strong gusts of wind blew our campsite and equipment right off the mountain.

Finding the ice cave in the middle of that storm was nothing short of a miracle, and there was no doubt in my mind that God had led me right to that shelter. When the snow parted into a tunnel, I was reminded of the story in the Bible of how God had parted the Red Sea for Moses and the Israelites so they could escape Pharoah and his Egyptian army. God was definitely in the business of miracles.

For the next three days, I huddled in that ice cave, hungry and severely hypothermic, while the blizzard raged outside. Before I had left for this trip, Alisa had shared with me that she'd had a nightmare of this very situation. But in her dream, I had frozen to death. I was determined *not* to let that happen.

I hoped that rescuers were on the way, but I honestly didn't know how they'd make it to us, or find me, in these conditions. In the meantime, all I could do was sit tight and wait.

But in addition to the physical battle of just staying

warm enough to survive, I was fighting spiritual battles, too.

"You're not a successful person. You're a drunk."

I shuddered. The words I heard were audible, and the voice was horrid. It was like a creepy, sinister, loud whisper in my ear.

"You're never going to be a good dad."

I felt sick to my stomach. I put my hands over my ears, trying to shut out the cutting insults.

"Take off your clothes and just die. Nobody will ever know."

I recognized the voice as one that could destroy me … I started thinking of it as Satan's. God's ultimate enemy. *My* ultimate enemy.

This went on for hours, every one of my insecurities being thrown in my face over and over again. This awful voice in my head knew exactly what my vulnerabilities were and hit every target without fail.

I realized right then and there that if God had a purpose for my life, it may also be true that something evil desired to end it. And if I did by chance end up surviving physically, the voice of doubt and despair was doing its best to make sure I was, at the very least, beaten mentally.

"You don't deserve Alisa. You're a failure as a husband."

Fight back.

But with what? Every man-made tool was gone and wouldn't help me against this attack, even if I had it. I bemoaned the fact that my Bible had been blown away with my tent. All I had was myself and my scant clothing in this dark icy cave in the middle of nowhere. I was so cold that it was hard for me to even think straight.

"You're worthless."

Fight back.

My mind was grasping for anything useful but kept coming up empty. And then, out of the blue, I remembered something so basic: a song I had learned in nursery school.

My lips were so frozen that I could barely form the words, but I raised my hoarse voice and sang with every ounce of energy that I could muster:

> *"Jesus loves me, this I know,*
> *For the Bible tells me so.*
> *Little ones to him belong;*
> *They are weak, but he is strong.*
> *Yes, Jesus loves me.*
> *Yes, Jesus loves me.*
> *Yes, Jesus loves me;*
> *The Bible tells me so."*

I sang it again and again. That song was the only weapon I had, but it was enough.

Then I heard another voice, but this one sounded like nothing I could ever even begin to describe. It filled the ice cave with its warmth and depth. I do believe it was the voice of God. "Brian," he said. "Everything he said you are, you are not. And everything he said you are not, you are."

Warm tears of thankfulness streamed down my face. And I knew that anything good in me was only because of God, anyway.

ৰেৰেৰে

On the third day, I was able to reach my friend in the Coast Guard on my satellite phone.

"The storm's too big," he said. "They are not attempting to get you guys. They believe it's going to be a body rescue. They are gathering next of kin and getting statements from the families. If you have any battery left on that satellite, you need to call your wife and say goodbye."

So I did. I called Alisa and told her how much I loved her and our sons.

"Honey, I'm not going to die here. I'm going to try to find the others, and if I die, it'll be while trying to get off this mountain."

With that, I re-entered the storm. I was already hungry, dehydrated and on the verge of frostbite. The storm was not quite as overpowering as it had been that first night, so I was able to find the other three guys and the shelter that they had built. And together, we walked down that mountain. It took a total of 11 hours for us to hike 21 miles through chest-deep snow. The skin between my legs was beginning to peel off. I collapsed several times from sheer exhaustion, but each time, I forced myself to get back up and keep going.

With every step, I just kept thinking about my beautiful wife and children. And I kept thinking about the battle in the ice cave at the summit of Sharatin Mountain that God and I had fought and won.

༺༒༻

A couple years later, I found myself on yet another mountaintop, where one of our company towers was located. A chopper had just dropped me off, and I quickly jogged toward the building that housed the generator, a layer of snow crunching beneath my boots.

Suddenly, I felt extreme pressure on my chest — like a hand stopping me.

Stop and look at the sunset, a voice in my head commanded.

Obediently, I stopped in my tracks. The sun was setting dramatically over the mountain peaks to the west of me, and the surrounding clouds were glowing bright orange and pink. The day's remaining light flickered over the valley below, casting long shadows as the sun sank lower in the sky. It was indeed a gorgeous sight.

But in the air above me, something shifted, and there was a loud cracking noise.

The tower!

I glanced up in time to see a massive slab of ice come loose from the tower and fall through the air, landing on the building below it and crushing it *flat*!

Holy crap!

I didn't even know what to think. If I had not stopped to watch the sunset, I'd be dead. And there was not a doubt in my mind that God had been the one to stop me.

Why all these close calls? Why all these narrow escapes?

I reached in my pocket for my cell phone and dialed my mom. I told her how God had spared my life yet again.

"What is *up* with my *life?*" I asked.

"Brian, there has been a battle over your life from the moment you were born. God's not done with you yet."

❧ ❧ ❧

I began to realize that my mom was right. Between my extreme sports, accidents, near-death experiences and addictions, I was a walking miracle, and I shouldn't have even been alive.

God had seen fit to preserve me through so many things, and I figured there must be a reason why.

Since I had decided to start living for Jesus, I needed to make sure that every part of my life lined up with what he wanted. He had done so much for me. More than anything, I wanted to please him.

Jesus, please show me what parts of me are okay and which parts need to go.

That was a difficult prayer to pray. But God showed me that he had created me to be an aggressive, intense person. He didn't want me to be any less that way. But he did want me to redirect it and take that same level of intensity into sharing his peace and hope with other people.

I had such compassion for people with addictions, so I started by volunteering with the Salvation Army. I went to homeless shelters, and I looked for people on the street. I remembered what it was like to be strung out, hopeless and waiting to die, so I made it my mission to find the people who were at the bottom of the barrel — who had completely given up. And when I found them, I asked God to give me the specific words they needed to hear.

Whenever I traveled on business in other cities, homeless people would approach me and ask me for money for food. I didn't want to give them money because I was afraid they would use it for alcohol or drugs. But I wanted with all my heart to help. The Bible is so clear on that:

> "For I was hungry and you gave me something to eat, I was thirsty and you gave me something to drink, I was a stranger and you invited me in, I needed clothes and you clothed me, I was sick and you looked after me, I was in prison and you came to visit me … Truly I tell you, whatever you did for one of the least of these brothers and sisters of mine, you did for me" (Matthew 25:35-40 NIV).

So I came up with a radical plan. I started carrying a backpack when I traveled, and I filled it with Bibles and power bars. The next time I was in Los Angeles, I parked my convertible Corvette rental car on the street and watched as a black guy on crack made his way down the sidewalk, asking everyone he saw for food. So I waited. When he finally stumbled toward me, I got out of the car and met him halfway.

"Hey, man, you got any food?"

Compassion for this man filled my being. I remembered what it was like to be hooked on coke.

"No, sir." I shook my head. "But I do have something better."

I reached into my backpack and handed him a Bible and power bar, neatly bundled together with a rubber band. Inside the Bible, though he hadn't opened it yet, was a note with these words: "For your body; for your soul. Peace be with you."

The man looked at me like I was crazy and muttered something unintelligible under his breath. I smiled back at him and watched as he moved on down the block, occasionally glancing over his shoulder at me. Maybe I hadn't given him what he wanted, but I knew I had given him what he needed.

At home, I became known among family and friends as one who would take on the most hopeless of addiction cases. When pastors had exhausted all means within the church while trying to help someone, they would call on me. I relied on God to give me the words to say to quickly break down walls people had built up in their minds and hearts.

The stories didn't all turn out with happy endings. I dealt with 20 heartbreaking suicides over the course of eight years of working with addicts.

What I had learned in my own life was that my addiction was a spiritual problem that required a spiritual solution. It was an inside job that only Jesus could fix. And I believed that no matter how far down someone had gone, it could still turn around into something more beautiful than could ever be imagined.

That truth alone, I believed, needed to be shared with anyone and everyone who would listen.

かかか

"You can do it, Jacob!"

The cheers for my 15-year-old son filled the bitter arctic air, and Alisa and I exchanged proud smiles. Our boys were competing in the Arctic Man competition in the Alaskan wilderness, and they were some of the youngest to participate.

Jacob stood on the edge of the ridge, rocking back and forth on his skis and looking intently at the course in front of him. Across the valley, our 13-year-old son, Joseph, sat on the snowmobile, waiting to meet Jacob at the bottom of the canyon and tow him up the next hill. The event was something we looked forward to every year. It was all about speed and perfect timing.

The start gun sounded, and Jacob was off down the slope at top speed, maneuvering each bump on the trail with great skill. As he skied out of view, I lifted my eyes to the lovely snowcapped peaks.

Thank you, Lord, for this beautiful world that my family and I enjoy.

Being a Christian was far from boring. In fact, every single day I was finding that living and doing what I believed God wanted me to do was one thrill after another — an adventure for my wildest dreams. I felt so undeserving.

Joy filled my heart. How could this be? How big is our God that he would match Alisa, one of the most radical female athletes in the valley, with me, one of the most radical of snowmobilers? And then God would combine our DNA within three gifted, athletic children? What kind of God do we serve that he would give a guy like me the kind of adrenaline-fueling job that I have, where I get to go to remote places that nobody has gone before?

The undeniable answer was this: a God who loves each and every unique one of us — a God who has a plan. A God who, in and of himself, is indeed *enough*.

THE MAN WHO WALKED WITHOUT A HEART

THE STORY OF NOAH

WRITTEN BY SHARON KIRK CLIFTON

The orca exploded from the water and pirouetted in the air before plunging back into the turquoise pool. I watched without seeing. Something wasn't right. I knew it, and my wife, Elizabeth, knew it. My heart had gone into arrhythmia as we walked to the Shamu show, but I tried to convince myself and Elizabeth that it would come out of it on its own. It always had.

Our two sons applauded along with the crowd as Shamu made a pass-by, scooping water with his tail and soaking everyone in the first few rows. Though we were sitting above the "splash zone," Elizabeth brushed away water from her cheek.

"Should we go?"

"No, no. The boys are loving this. I'll be fine."

Concern marked her face. Hoping to reassure her, I slipped my arm around her shoulders. She didn't look convinced.

"Dear, I'm fine. I expect my heart will go back in normal sinus rhythm soon." I tried to muster a smile, but she wasn't buying it. "You're missing your favorite part of the show. Look. The trainer is about to surf on Shamu's back."

"Noah, you're pale."

"Too much sun block."

"Stop. I'm going to get you some help." She stood to leave.

"Please no, Elizabeth. It'll pass, just as it did the last time. Let the boys enjoy the show."

She pursed her lips and settled down onto the bleacher. "Just as soon as this is over …"

Finally, Shamu took his last bow. Elizabeth took off — our sons in tow — to get help. The stands emptied. I couldn't stay where I was. The clean-up crew swept in like a summer thunderstorm to ready the stadium for the next show. I walked in the direction Elizabeth had gone. *Take it slow*, I told myself. *Sit down, if needed.*

My breathing was shallow. When I tried to suck air into my lungs, it seemed to stop somewhere shy of my Adam's apple. I could feel my heart pounding in an irregular staccato.

I had been through this before, prior to the trip. A doctor put me on a treadmill and noticed some ventricular tachycardia, rapid heartbeats, but they self-corrected quickly. I hadn't felt them. Over the next few months, however, I had a couple more incidents that I did feel.

I certainly felt it now. The farther I walked, the weaker I became. I thanked God it was November and not August. The added burden of heat and humidity would have been too much. I welcomed the sight of Elizabeth and some paramedics power-walking toward me. Some part of my brain noticed the boys weren't with them. Elizabeth told me later she had left them with the Sea World nurse.

A minute later, I was the center of a flurry of activity. The paramedics gave me the once-over, checking blood pressure, temperature and pulse.

One person stood like a rock apart from the others, hand over her mouth, eyes closed, brows knitted together. I knew she was praying.

"Elizabeth." She opened her eyes. "It's okay." I got the words out before they slipped an oxygen mask over my face.

She nodded.

"Pulse 220," said the medic who checked my vital signs. "He's arrhythmic. Ventricular tachycardia. He shouldn't even be conscious, let alone up and walking." It's not a good sign when they talk about you in the third person and you're right there.

❧❧❧

The medical team rushed me to the hospital, where I was diagnosed with idiopathic dilated cardiomyopathy (IDC) — Latin for "this man's heart is in really bad shape." I had to be shocked three times to jump me out of the dangerous arrhythmia.

How could this be happening? I was only 39 years old. I followed a healthy diet, and Elizabeth and I walked nearly every day, no matter the weather. Though my career as lead instrument technician for an oil company on Alaska's North Slope kept me on the road a lot and put me in contact with people, I seldom got so much as a sniffle. And suddenly I had this life-threatening condition. It didn't make sense. We believed that God allows things to happen for a purpose, but I saw no purpose in this.

The Florida doctors made it clear I wouldn't be traveling home right away. I needed an internal defibrillator, since the arrhythmias were serious enough to cause sudden death. Following the surgery, Elizabeth and I agreed that we should send the boys home to Wasilla, Alaska, so they could continue school. We had a large family there to care for them, and we knew our friends would help in any way they could.

When we were able to return to Wasilla, I started seeing a new doctor who prescribed a regimen of various anti-arrhythmic and heart-failure medications.

ﾍﾟﾍﾟﾍﾟ

Over the next few years, I felt as though my heart was a battleground. It often went wild and required a shock from the internal defibrillator to bring it into a normal rhythm. I got to where I could sense a shock coming, and I would brace for it, knowing that afterward, I would feel better immediately.

Once, following a shock, Elizabeth asked me how I felt.

"Like I just got punched in the chest," I said, "but I'm

feeling much better now that my heart is beating normally."

Elizabeth took my hand. "Noah, you're my hero."

"I don't feel like a hero."

"Well, you are. I don't know very many people who would stay so upbeat in this situation. You're definitely a 'glass-half-full' sort of guy."

"We know God is in control. None of this comes as a surprise to him."

At one point, the defibrillator shock didn't work to normalize my heart, and I had to be transported by Medevac to the University of Washington Medical Center in Seattle. Doctors there tried another treatment, but it also failed, so they put me on a powerful anti-arrhythmic drug known for some nasty side effects. When I developed thyroid problems, the result of the strong med, I had to stop taking it.

We never ceased praying, knowing God could heal me completely without any further medical intervention, if he chose. We'd seen it happen to others. If he didn't want to give me a spontaneous healing, if he wanted to go another route, that would be fine, too.

The dozen years following our November 1999 Florida vacation-turned-nightmare passed in a blur of doctor consultations, hospital runs and surgeries to replace or upgrade the internal defibrillator. I could have written a tour guide of Alaska's leading medical facilities. Providence Alaska Medical Center, Mat-Su Regional Medical Center, Central Peninsula General Hospital,

Alaska Heart Institute — Elizabeth and I got to know them all as we battled not only arrhythmia but also the consequences of my erratic heart: edema and blood clots.

Meanwhile, I kept working at my job on Alaska's North Slope. I remained physically active, also. Elizabeth and I continued to take our long walks. Friends who knew I used a defibrillator often commented on my activity level.

"How can you do all you do?" they'd ask, or, "Should you still be hiking for miles? Is that even good for you?"

If the heart event in Florida had any positive effect on my life at all, it was to cement my determination to be *more* active. Whatever the future held, I wanted to face it as physically strong as possible.

So we walked.

ক্তক্তক্ত

In 2006, we adopted a hobby that took our hiking to a new level: geocaching, an international game of hide-and-seek where players try to locate hidden containers using a smart phone or GPS. We loved these adventures because they took us to places we might not otherwise go, sites the average tourist didn't know about. I've always been an outdoorsman, but our geocache quests made our hiking all the more interesting.

On May 20, 2011, Gracie entered our lives. She was a blonde golden retriever puppy who wiggled and yipped her way into our hearts quickly. Golden retrievers are generally intelligent, empathetic, gentle and faithful — characteristics that make them the number one choice for service dogs. Elizabeth immediately began training her. Gracie went everywhere with us, including on geocache excursions. She was our golden shadow.

In January 2012, the situation with my heart worsened. Pumping capacity dropped significantly, and because the blood wasn't being pumped through my heart fast enough, I was getting clots in the ventricles. My doctor at Alaska Heart Institute recommended I consult specialists at the University of Washington Medical Center (UDub) in Seattle to see if I would be a good candidate for a heart transplant.

One night, prior to our flight to Seattle, I had a vivid dream. I saw a stainless-steel tray like one would see in an operating room. The tray held my heart and pacemaker/defibrillator, along with the wires needed to make it work. Was I engaging in wishful thinking, or was there a deeper meaning? Was it just a dream, or was God trying to tell me something? I interpreted it to mean my native heart would be healed. Perhaps UDub would have some answers.

As we walked through UDub's doors on January 24, 2012, I took Elizabeth's hand. "Ready for this next step on our journey?"

Concern etched her face as she set her jaw and nodded.

"We'll have to work fast," I said. "We're only here for a couple days."

Or so we thought.

❧❧❧

I spent the day going from lab to lab and on to the next lab. Finally, we met with Dr. White. When she entered the conference room, her face was somber. She scanned a stack of pages on her clipboard before introducing herself and shaking our hands.

"Noah, looking at the results of today's labs, it's amazing you're alive." When neither Elizabeth nor I said anything, she continued. "I see your home is in Wasilla, Alaska. Correct?"

"Yes," I said.

"So you flew here?"

"Yes."

"You cannot fly home. We're not sure you would even survive the trip."

I heard Elizabeth's intake of breath.

I cleared my throat. "But our family is expecting us. We have two sons —"

"I don't like to put it like this, but I must make you realize … death is imminent."

Elizabeth reached for my hand. I took hers and squeezed.

"So what can we do?" she asked in a voice barely above a whisper.

"For starters, we need to admit you today so we can treat the heart failure. I know you've been through a lot today, but we need to run more tests to see if you are a candidate for a heart transplant. Then we need to discuss installing an LVAD."

"LVAD?" I said.

"Yes. A left ventricular assist device. It's a kind of mechanical heart, but not really a replacement heart. It helps your native heart do its job. It does have certain risks, however."

"Like what?" Elizabeth said.

"It has been associated with stroke, bleeding and infection. And, of course, it is a mechanical device, so it can simply fail. We'll do everything possible to make sure none of those things happen. As with any surgery, there's always risk."

I was admitted to the hospital. Once I was settled in my room, Elizabeth came in. Her eyes were red-rimmed. She had either been crying or was fighting back tears.

"Noah, I can't do this."

"Yes, Elizabeth, you can. Is Philippians 4:13 no longer true?"

"What do you mean?"

"The verse. 'I can do all things through Christ who strengthens me' (NKJV). Are there new limitations on that?"

"You know what I mean."

"No, Elizabeth. Tell me."

She began pacing around the room. "Seattle's a big city, Noah. But somehow I've got to find my way around it without you. You always do the big city driving. And what about a car? I've got to get one. And a place to live, because don't you think for one minute I'm going home to Wasilla and leave you here. And that stupid GPS. I don't know how to use it. You always do that. *You*, Noah!" She folded her arms and turned to look out at the panorama of the UDub campus.

I watched her back and waited until the tension released from her shoulders. "You're right," I said. She turned to face me, but said nothing. "You can't do it, but Christ can, dear."

Her lips formed a tight line as she nodded. "I know."

"Think about it, Elizabeth. Who has been my co-pilot on all our geocaching adventures?"

"Gracie." It was good to see her smile again.

"Okay, I'll give you that one. But you're next in line after Gracie. And the GPS isn't really that complicated. Besides it'll talk to you."

"Goody."

"You don't have to figure it all out today. You can start tomorrow and take it one step at a time."

"I guess."

"Come sit down." I nodded to the chair beside the bed. "Something else concerns me."

"What?"

"My dream. This LVAD thing doesn't align with the dream at all because both the LVAD and my native heart would be in my chest. Right?"

"Uh, yeah. I think so."

"So that can't be the answer, not if the dream was from God."

THE MAN WHO WALKED WITHOUT A HEART

❧ ❧ ❧

Over a two-week period, while I underwent every kind of test and evaluation known to man, or so it seemed, Elizabeth, the woman who had a mini-meltdown at the idea of taking on Seattle, accomplished amazing things. She found a car that suited our needs, secured a rental apartment and arranged to borrow some furniture.

"Elizabeth, you're my hero," I said after she added that she was almost comfortable with the GPS.

"Why do you say that?"

"You're one courageous lady. I'm glad you're on my team."

As the lab results made their way to the various specialists, they came in to discuss them. The news was never good, so we got to where we dreaded seeing them come.

One day, the hematologist, a woman, came in and pronounced the most dire declaration of all. "Your blood workup shows it is likely you have leukemia." Considering the state of my heart, wasn't this a death sentence? My grandfather had died of leukemia. What now? Would that automatically disqualify me for a transplant? It seemed likely, because they would hardly transplant a donor heart in someone with … "We won't know for sure until we take a bone marrow sample. I'll schedule that."

Elizabeth looked as stricken as I felt. I tried not to let my own feelings reflect in my expression. Having dropped the "L" bomb, the hematologist left us alone to clear away the destruction.

"Oh, Noah, what now?"

"Dear, she said they don't know for sure. They won't until they test the bone marrow."

My two sisters — one from Arizona and one from Southeast Alaska — had come to be with us for a few days. When they got to the hospital, the four of us prayed for answers and healing.

The bone marrow test ruled out leukemia. Either the initial test was wrong or God healed me. We were thrilled either way.

෴

Dr. Connor, the co-director of heart transplantation, came by to tell us I had been approved as a candidate for a heart transplant.

"Meanwhile," he said, "we must address the immediate problem. Your edema is controlled, but honestly, Noah, neither I nor my colleagues have ever seen someone function as well as you with a 6 percent ejection fraction." By now, I had become familiar with the heart and its terminology. Normal ejection fractions of the left ventricle, the heart's main pumping chamber, are 55 to 70 percent, since the ventricles never empty completely. I was on blood thinners to lower the risk of more clots. "How can you even be alive?"

I shot a quick glance at Elizabeth, and she winked at

me. "So, they've talked to me about the LVAD," I said. "Is that the next step while we wait for a donor heart?"

Dr. Connor shook his head. "Absolutely not. There is no way I would put an LVAD in you. You have biventricular failure. Your right ventricle is too weak, and it's not going to provide adequate flow to that left ventricular assist device. The only thing I will put in you at this point is a total artificial heart."

Elizabeth shifted in her chair. "So ... what all does that entail?"

"Cutting out the ventricles and four heart valves and replacing all that with a polyurethane pump — two bulbous ventricles that are held together with Velcro. The Velcro makes the artificial heart adjustable to the chest cavity."

Dr. Connor went on to describe the conventional practice at that time. In order to function, the TAH would be hooked up to a cumbersome 418-pound compressor known as "Big Blue," unless I was willing to participate in a manufacturer's trial of a 13-pound compressor called a Freedom Driver. The device, developed by SynCardia, was quite portable.

Elizabeth and I looked at one another in silence. I wrestled with the idea of having my native heart sliced out and replaced with a plastic one. The Freedom Driver, however, made the possibility more feasible. I tented my fingers under my chin. "Limitations?"

"Only battery life. Which is why you want to have two sets. The batteries are good for about two hours. You'd want to be careful not to get too far away from a recharging source. It can recharge from a car battery outlet or any AC outlet. Of course, you will have two tubes from your chest that connect to the driver. Anything like that poses a risk of infection. And it's loud. You still interested? Shall I schedule the procedure?"

"This is a lot to absorb. I need some time to think about it, you know, talk it over."

"You don't have a lot of time, Noah. Over the past 12 years, the internal defibrillators have delivered 30 shocks to bring your heart back into normal rhythm. Your native heart is weakening rapidly. But I understand your wanting to talk it over with your wife. I'll get back to you. Meanwhile, I'll go ahead and schedule the O.R."

Dr. Connor left, and Elizabeth went to get my sisters. Again we gathered in the room and prayed for a spontaneous healing by God, so I wouldn't need the artificial heart. After the amens, Elizabeth sank into a chair. "I've come to a conclusion."

"Yes," I said. "And what is that?"

"We've been praying that God would heal you, right? Without more surgery. Right? We all agree he could do that. But he has his own way of doing things. What if his way of healing you, Noah, is with this artificial heart, at least while we wait for a donor heart? Life and death still are in his hands. Through the past dozen years, he's used the ventricular defibrillators to keep your native heart in line. Are they less of a miracle because they're mechanical?"

THE MAN WHO WALKED WITHOUT A HEART

"I just want to know God's will," I said, but I continued to struggle with the idea of forfeiting my native heart. UDub had installed such a heart only two times before, both in January 2012.

Neither patient had survived.

❧ ❧ ❧

I was a common sight in the halls as I loped through my laps, usually with Elizabeth by my side. We racked up many miles. Some of the other doctors questioned the wisdom of implanting an artificial heart versus an LVAD because I appeared to be doing so well. Hospital staff members smiled as they passed us, shaking their heads. I was the aberrant patient they'd heard about.

One day, as I trekked along by myself, I went into a severe ventricular tachycardia. I felt it coming on, so I reached out for the wall and slid to my knees. I was attached to an I.V. pole. Suddenly my world faded to black. When I regained consciousness, the I.V. pole was tipped over, and I was surrounded by people. The internal defibrillator had failed to shock my heart, but the heart had come out of the arrhythmia on its own.

I had prayed for direction, and this was it. Dr. Connor had tentatively scheduled O.R. for the next day, February 6, 2012, so he installed the total artificial heart then. My dream had been fulfilled, though I was sedated, of course, and didn't see the native heart and defibrillator laying in a metal tray.

Everything seemed to be going well following surgery, until six days later when things began to spiral downward. I felt horrible. I had cardiac tamponade, fluid around the artificial heart causing severe pressure, and I was in bad shape.

I vaguely remember Elizabeth leaning over me, kissing my temple and whispering in my ear. "Noah, tell your spirit to fight. Do you hear me? Dear, dear Noah, TELL YOUR SPIRIT TO FIGHT!"

The surgeon rushed in and said he had to open me up again. Immediately!

After the operation, the surgeon told Elizabeth I had been without oxygen for some time and might have suffered organ or brain damage. Hearing that, Elizabeth called our pastor's wife. It was Sunday, and church was in session. Nonetheless, the pastor's wife answered her cell phone. We learned later that the congregation stopped what they were doing to pray for me. God heard those prayers. I had no damage resulting from the tamponade.

Of course, I was eager to leave the hospital.

"What's your opinion of paparazzi?" said Dr. Connor. Neither Elizabeth nor I expected that question. "I ask because there will be a press conference, since you'll be making history. When you walk out the front door of UW pulling the Freedom Driver, you'll be the first person discharged from UW to do so."

"Is that necessary? I'm not one to seek the limelight."

"It can't be avoided, I'm afraid. Your leaving the hospital with the Freedom Driver will be a very big moment. Besides, your story can give hope to others dealing with similar challenges."

Elizabeth and I agreed it would be worth treading through a sea of cameras and reporters if we could help others, if this device granted mobility to those awaiting heart transplants.

Finally, the day came for me to leave the hospital. March 21, 2012. I was ready to go to the apartment Elizabeth had rented — "home" while we awaited a donor heart, however long that might be. We endured the press conference with the help of the hospital's device coordinator, Anna.

❧❧❧

Elizabeth made arrangements for Gracie to be flown down to Seattle while I was recovering in the hospital from the total artificial heart surgery. We both missed her and knew she missed us. She wasn't 2 yet — still a pup — and our adventures in Seattle had interrupted her training. Elizabeth was eager to get started again on that.

We enrolled Gracie in an obedience school. Both Elizabeth and I attended. The instructor saw me as a training tool for the animals, so they became accustomed to the *whump-uh-tuh*, *whump-uh-tuh*, *whump-uh-tuh*, *whump-uh-tuh* of the Freedom Driver.

❧❧❧

While I had kept up my walking in the polished halls of UDub, it had been more than two months since I had hiked outdoors, longer since we'd geocached. We both were eager to get back into our routine, even if it had to be a truncated version to accommodate battery life. The rhythm of the Freedom Driver marked the cadence of our treks.

On one of our hikes in early April, I stopped to breathe, not because I was short of breath, not because my heart was arrhythmic, but because it was spring in Washington. A light rain had fallen that morning, and the fragrance of blossoms opening to the fresh sun permeated everything.

"Are you all right, Noah?" Before the artificial heart, such stops were a sign of distress.

I inhaled deeply. "Smell that?"

She flared her nostrils like a fox testing the air. "What is it?"

"Creation. Rain. Flowers. Freedom. Maybe that's today's geocache."

"Could be." She picked up a stick and tossed it. "Gracie, fetch! Go get it, girl." Gracie took off after the stick, retrieved it and brought it back to Elizabeth.

I checked the battery meter. "Guess we should go ahead and swap out the batteries." We were thankful for the Freedom Driver, but we anticipated the day when I'd have a new heart and we wouldn't have to worry about dying batteries.

Over the spring and summer, we trekked 607 miles. I

wanted to make sure I was in top-notch physical condition when that call came that a donor heart had been found. During that time, we located many geocaches.

I had to climb a tree to retrieve one cache. When Anna, the device coordinator, called later to check in and see how everything was going, Elizabeth told her about that little adventure. I hadn't planned to mention it.

"Noah," Anna said, "don't even tell me what you're doing. And I'm not going to tell you what not to do because you'll take it as a challenge and do it." Some people in similar situations would be content to sit around home, watch TV and wait for "the call." I couldn't do that. I wanted to live.

Throughout this 13-year journey, Elizabeth and I frequently sat down to catch our breath and think about how God had been with us every step of the way, even when things weren't going as we thought they should.

Before the first heart event, back in 1999, God began preparing us for the geocache of a lifetime. If he hadn't, this adventure would have bankrupted us. I had never budgeted. I earned a decent living and didn't see the need until I heard Dave Ramsey, whose financial planning program based on Biblical principles has helped many people. I wanted to eliminate consumer debt and save purposefully. I bought the DVD set, and Elizabeth and I listened to them. When we had to set up a household in Seattle while maintaining our Wasilla home, we had a fully-funded emergency account. Some of my coworkers contributed to a special fund, also, which helped a lot.

I grew up in a Christian family and decided to follow Jesus Christ when I was a boy. If I really am a glass-half-full man, it's because I learned early on that God knows what he's doing. Nothing comes as a surprise to him. The events of the past few years have taught me that he is a very personal God whom we can trust completely. Psalm 27 in the Bible became especially meaningful for both Elizabeth and me at this time, especially verse 14.

> "Wait for the LORD; be strong,
> and let your heart take courage;
> Wait for the LORD" (ESV).

So we waited.

❧❧❧

The phone rang. I answered. It was Anna.

"Noah, you sitting down?"

"Yes. Is this it?"

"Yes. We have a heart for you."

I glanced over my shoulder at Elizabeth. She had both hands clamped over her mouth. Though she was hearing only my end of the conversation, she obviously surmised what the call was about.

"Are you sure?" I said.

"I'm sure." Since I didn't say anything, Anna continued. "Do you need to put Elizabeth on so I can tell her?"

"No, I'll be able to tell her. Wow."

"Wow, indeed. Get to the hospital as quickly as possible."

I hung up the phone, and Elizabeth and I hurried to get packed and out the door. The call had come at about 7:30 p.m. By 9 p.m., we were at the hospital. By 10:30 a.m., Wednesday, September 12, 2012, I was in surgery to receive my new heart.

Elizabeth was not allowed to be in the operating room, but she did wish she could see what the scene looked like. A photographer took photos for her, including one that showed the donor heart lying in a stainless-steel tray.

"Oh, Noah, it's totally a miracle," she said later. "God is so good. Thank you, Jesus!"

We stayed in Seattle for three months to be near UDub. Dr. White kept close tabs on me, watching out for any signs of rejection, but the anti-rejection drugs did their job well. Finally, in December, we gave away our Seattle furniture to some college students and shipped our car and other belongings home. We arrived in Wasilla on December 20.

Just in time for Christmas.

❧❧❧

Christmas 2012 was quiet. Because of the risk of infection, I couldn't be in crowds. It was enough, though, to be home with family, friends and our Northgate Alaska church family nearby.

After a breakfast of cold cereal, Elizabeth and I went for our usual hike. It had snowed before we returned from Seattle, and a mantle of white still covered the farm fields along our path. The sky provided a cerulean backdrop for alabaster mountain peaks.

A handful of chickadees hopped among a tangle of berry briars, having discovered some remaining morsels.

"Look, Noah." Elizabeth pointed overhead to where a bald eagle soared silently.

"Guess he's looking for breakfast," I said.

Gracie barked at the eagle, then took off. She made a game of bounding ahead, turning to face us and waiting until we caught up.

As we climbed one moderate hill, I could hear my heart beating. It was a little fast because of the exertion, but it was regular.

Because I don't have my native heart, the vagus nerve can no longer perform one of its functions: to slow the heart when needed. I have to wait for the heart to regulate its speed on its own.

After we'd trekked a couple miles, we turned toward home. Fragrant wood smoke from fireplaces drifted on the air, mingling occasionally with that of roasting ham and other cooking smells. At some houses, cars filled driveways and lined streets as families gathered for the celebration. Normally, that would be us, but not this year.

Later in the afternoon, Elizabeth drove me to my parents' home. Then she went to spend a couple hours with her family. I couldn't accompany her there because it was a large gathering. She stayed a short time, but soon joined me. After dinner, we went home.

As our quiet Christmas drew to a close, we settled down on the couch to watch some TV. Elizabeth pulled the afghan from the back of the couch and threw it over our laps. Gracie strolled into the room, stretched and yawned and lay across my feet.

"God's Faithful Grace," I said, calling Gracie by her full name, "you're one good dog."

Elizabeth reached down to scratch Gracie between her ears. Then she rested her head on my shoulder. "God's grace is faithful."

"Sure is. We don't deserve all the good things he gives us, but he keeps on giving."

"Merry Christmas, Noah."

"Merry Christmas, dear."

DREAMER

The Story of Savannah
Written by Angela Welch Prusia

Small orbs of light danced around the room. They spiraled and dipped, flitting through the air like fireflies on a midsummer night.

I gazed at their sparkly reflection in my grandmother's ornate mirror while she plaited my long blond hair. My parents had left for work before I'd awoken.

"Liebchen." Her thick German broke my trance. "What are you dreaming about?"

"Do you see them, Oma?" I pointed to the chest of drawers. A light rested on the corner, and another blinked near the bronze handle of the top drawer.

Her blue eyes twinkled. "See what, little loved one?"

"The flying lights."

She shook her head and tied off my braid. "There's nothing here, child. Just you and me." She patted my head. "Go outside to play, little dreamer."

❧❧❧

"Why are you upset, Oma?" I wrapped my arms around my grandmother's thick waist.

"You're my world." She sniffled. "I'm not ready for you to leave, Liebchen."

I kissed her hand and smelled baby powder and the familiar cardamom spice she used in many of her recipes. I didn't want to move. Eight years of memories filled this home in the suburbs in the California Bay area.

She caressed my cheek. "You'll love life in the country. Your parents have saved so hard to build their dream house."

The new place loomed in my mind. The five bedrooms and large square-foot area would only widen the distance between the three of us. Oma kissed my scrapes and bruises and tucked me in at night. I barely knew the strangers called my parents.

Tears blurred my vision. "I don't want a new home. I want to live with you."

"I'll call you every day." She held me. "Castro Valley is just 30 miles away. We'll visit each other all the time."

"Promise?"

My grandmother put on a brave smile. "Do you promise? You'll be so busy riding Dolly, you might forget ol' Oma."

My new sorrel quarter horse was my only consolation. I squeezed my grandmother.

"I'll never forget you, Oma."

❧❧❧

"What's this mess?" My father swallowed a shot of whiskey. "Our guests will be arriving soon."

I cowered in the corner. I'd forgotten to clean up after

I'd made myself lunch, and the weekend meant parties thrown by my parents.

"Come here!" he bellowed.

I stepped forward, bracing myself for the blows. Ten years in Hitler's youth camps had hardened my father. He rarely spoke about those days which shadowed his life in pain and disillusionment.

From fragments of conversations, I knew that he'd been taken from his parents at age 5. By 14, he'd been driving a tank in the Panzer Division when the war ended. He'd immigrated to America not long after.

My cries filled the room, but my mother didn't look up from her jigsaw puzzle. Unlike Oma, she spent her days watching soap operas. She'd quit her job at the telephone company to take care of the baby. He took what affection she had. I was nothing more than an afterthought.

෭෮෮෮

Not long after our move, the neighbors welcomed us. Judd hit it off with my father and invited him to join a service club.

"And what's your name, pretty girl?" He knelt beside me and touched my hand.

"I'm Savannah." I practiced the manners taught me by my grandmother. "It's nice to meet you, Mister."

"Call me Uncle Judd." His eyes bore into me, so that I looked down at my feet. "I'm sure we'll become great friends."

The wolf began grooming me with small gifts and unexpected visits. Starved for attention, I easily became trapped in his lair.

❧❧❧

Beady eyes leered at me from under the bed.

"You're mine," the monster rasped, choking me with his foul breath.

"Stay back!" I hugged my knees.

The monster grasped at the air with grizzly hands. Long yellow fingernails caked with dirt yanked at the bed skirt, pulling me closer.

I forced open my eyes.

Beside me, Uncle Judd snored loudly. I clutched the covers, pulling them over my nakedness. The wolf had lured me to his bed.

Someone sat in the corner. Tears streaked his gentle features, pooling in the purest eyes I'd ever seen. I stared into their depths and couldn't bear the sorrow and pain he carried. He cried for me.

I knew the man. Jesus. I'd seen pictures of him at the church where my mom dropped me off. But the people there seemed more concerned with their rituals and traditions. No one talked about that part of me who envisioned things. My earliest memories were dreams. Even now at the age of 9, I knew there was more to me than skin and bones. If Jesus was their god, I wanted nothing to do with him.

Jesus held out his arms, beckoning me to come to him. But I dismissed him. I was a spirit born of the earth.

ھو ھو ھو

"Come on, girl." I nudged Dolly through the trees and into the clearing. The sun warmed my bare arms and legs. We'd been gone all day, but I wouldn't be missed.

Dolly stopped. She had an ornery streak and knew how to manipulate me.

"Okay," I agreed. "We'll take a break."

I slid off the saddle and rubbed the soft hair on her neck.

"Savannah?" A familiar voice reached my ears.

"Hey, Peter," I greeted one of the kids who rode my bus. He tied up his horse, and we sat in the grass, sharing a bottle of brandy. I'd been drinking for years, encouraging myself that it was part of my German heritage.

I lay back against Peter's leg and stared at the clouds floating overhead. Dolly chomped on tufts of grass. Peter traced a finger down my arm and lifted my shirt. Uncle Judd had discarded me not long after I turned 12, and after four years of his attentions, I'd been stripped of any sense of self-value. I viewed myself as he did — an object, worth only what my body could offer. I gave myself to Peter.

And Roger.

And Johnny.

And Bill.

I lost track of their names. My mom didn't even flinch when I demanded a prescription for birth control when I turned 14.

The emptiness only grew. To numb the pain, I stole my father's alcohol and regularly got drunk by the time the school bus rolled into the parking lot. I missed many classes due to my frequent hangovers, so my grades suffered. I turned to drugs and the occult. Anything to make me feel alive.

෴෴෴

"Who's this sweet thang?" Jerry's eyes lingered on my legs where my miniskirt ended.

"Savannah." Flower introduced me to her older friend. She was in her 20s, a fun-loving hippie I'd met who'd been teaching me to drive.

We spent the afternoon talking and flirting. The next day, he brought me flowers.

"What are these for?" I grinned at Jerry.

He pecked me on the cheek. "Can't a guy get flowers for a wonderful girl?"

I tried not to squeal. I didn't want to look like a foolish schoolgirl. Jerry brought me more gifts, and I gave him my body in return.

"Be home by curfew," I called out to my mom one Saturday. The car keys jingled in my hands. She never asked about my new boyfriend.

Alcohol slurred Jerry's speech when I pulled up at his

place. I hated to see him drunk because he got mean, so I tried to take away the bottle.

"Don't take my booze, you worthless slut." Jerry backhanded me. I touched the stinging skin, eyes wide with surprise.

Rage fueled him. He beat me until bruises covered my body.

After the assault, he fell asleep. I slipped into the bathroom and cleaned up the blood. I slumped in a corner and let the tears run down my face.

Jesus appeared before me, holding out his hands. I turned to the wall in shame. *How could God love someone like me?*

Jerry woke from his stupor, and I flinched in fear.

"Baby, what happened?" He leaned over me and kissed a bruise on my arm.

I moaned, and he wrapped his arms around me. "Did I hurt you?"

How could he not remember?

"You gotta forgive me, babe," Jerry pleaded. "I'm so sorry."

కొడుకు

The pattern continued with Jerry until I fully believed his lies. He completely broke me only to reshape me. His every wish became my desire. When Jerry ran out of drug and alcohol money, he sold me to his friends. We married when I turned 18 and soon had a son and a daughter.

When Gabby turned 2, I realized I couldn't subject my kids to Jerry's rages any longer. I could take the abuse myself, but watching my kids suffer tore my heart apart. I filed for divorce, and Jerry didn't waste time finding another doormat.

Jerry refused to work so he wouldn't have to pay child support, and I lost the house. I found work at a boarding stable, where the owners let me and the kids sleep in the two-room office. We lay toe-to-toe on a single couch surrounded by tools and office supplies, the whinny of the horses lulling us to sleep. With no running water and the ever-present stench of horse manure, the conditions were less than ideal for a toddler and a preschooler, but I saw no better choice. When their bellies rumbled with hunger, I sold myself for food. Every day meant a battle to survive.

૭ૐ૭ૐ૭ૐ

Roy walked into my life like a kiss from heaven. Four years younger than me, the rugged cowboy I met at a rodeo promised to rescue me. I wanted to pinch myself when he took me and the kids to live on his family's ranch. I had to be dreaming again.

I loved life on the ranch. I rode the horses all over the sprawling terrain surrounded by redwoods and teeming with wildlife. Work at an AIDS clinic and later at a preschool gave me purpose, but the damage from my past demanded attention. I practiced Wiccan and cast spells in an attempt to change my circumstances. My outlook turned extremely pessimistic. Between my negativity and life with kids, Roy began to distance himself. After one fight, he took the generator out of the fifth-wheel trailer where we lived on the ranch.

"It's snowing." I pointed outside. "Me and the kids are going to freeze."

Roy's temple throbbed. "Go ahead. If you leave, don't bother coming back."

What choice did I have? I bundled up my shivering babies and took the four-wheel drive into town. Tears blurred my vision, making it difficult to drive. I loved Roy. His rejection added to my growing pile.

Jesus showed up again, holding out his hands, but I wouldn't even look at him.

꙳꙳꙳

A friend encouraged me to become a carpenter, so I joined the union. My brother took the kids while I slept on a cot in a tool shed on my mom's property. I showered in the house, but her new husband wouldn't let me stay with them. I counted the days until I qualified for a low-rent apartment and could reunite with the kids.

My small stature enabled me to scale the metal frames on the skyscrapers we built, so the guys took me under their wing. They helped with any heavy lifting and protected me from predators, like my boss. I traded my body for food or new clothes, but I wouldn't commit to a relationship.

❧❧❧

"I'm sorry," the principal at my daughter's private school told me behind closed doors. "If you can't pay the tuition, she will have to be transferred."

"But I can't put her in public schools," I pleaded. "She'll never make it." Gabby needed extra attention for learning issues.

"I wish there was something I could offer."

I rested my head in my hands, worn out from trying to find a solution. Life was a struggle just to keep food on the table. *How could I help my daughter?*

"What about other states?" I asked. "Are there better programs offered in public schools?"

"If you're willing to move." She raised her eyebrows. "Washington State and Alaska are two of the best."

That night I dreamed of Alaska.

❧❧❧

I loaded the last of our things into my Toyota truck and wiped the sweat from my brow.

"Be good for Grandma." I kissed Gabby. "Mom and Joshua will see you in a few weeks after we find a place to stay."

Casey, our Australian Shepherd, jumped in beside me, and we hit the road. George Strait crooned from the speakers. "Alaska, here we come."

Scenes from my dream unfolded as we drove on gravel

roads and slept in the truck bed at night, a pistol under my head to protect us from bears and other unwanted predators. I didn't know exactly what to expect, but at least my dreams confirmed the path.

કે કે કે

"What brings you to Alaska?" Jed asked a month later as I refilled his mug with coffee. Steam curled to the rafters mixing with the smell of eggs and hash browns on the grill.

"My kid." I circled the table at the diner and topped off coffees for the rest of the group. This ragtag bunch of grandpas had quickly warmed their way into my heart. "She needs a special school, and her teachers pointed me to Alaska."

"Little different from the weather in sunny California, huh?" Micah gave a humpf. His plaid shirt was worn at the collar.

I set the pot back on the warmer and grabbed a tub to clean an empty table nearby. "Yeah, but I love the land. I can't wait till I finish our house."

"Who's your contractor?" Rusty leaned back in his chair.

"Me."

I nearly got a coffee bath. The men sputtered their surprise. Droplets of brown liquid beaded on bushy beards.

Clyde recovered first. "You're building a house?"

I nodded, dumping a piece of half-eaten toast off a chipped plate into the bus tub. Orange juice left a ring in the bottom of a glass. "I'm a carpenter."

"No way." Jed whistled. "You're too scrawny."

"It's true." I laughed, unoffended. "Want to see my union card?"

I took the tub of dirty dishes back to the dishwasher. Their voices carried through the diner.

"I got a job for you, then," Clyde said. "A buddy of mine is looking for help with a shed."

I wiped my hands on my apron. "Great. Give him my name."

Soon my coffee regulars became my greatest advertisers.

❧❧❧

"So how much do I owe you?" Justin asked. We were in the basement of his rental business after hours, another job from my coffee crew.

"Nothing." I finished my Coke and helped him put the tools away. "You built the shelves."

"But I hired you." He kissed my neck.

"And you did all the work." I wrapped my hands around his waist.

"Which is why I need a break."

I giggled as he kissed me again.

"Move in with me."

I thought about my cozy apartment above the diner. It

would be months till my house would be finished. I agreed. This time, my relationship with Justin wasn't founded on my need for rescue. Life would be different. Better.

Four months later, we married. We finished the house and moved in before winter hit. The baby came two years after that.

≈≈≈

I thought things with Justin would be different than my other failed relationships, but reality proved different. Bitterness clung to me, while anger lurked under my every mood. Justin and I fought. Justin's daughter and I fought. Dysfunction ruled our home. Divorce came up in every conversation for the next 15 years, but staying together was less complicated. We settled into living separate lives under the same roof.

When a close friend's 8-year-old daughter died in an accident, fear gripped me in a strangling hold.

My children boarded the bus in the mornings for school, and I followed behind, watching until they made it safely inside. Every mention of death and disease terrified me. I stopped reading the mysteries I once devoured. I cried at everything. Control slipped from my life like sand through an hourglass.

≈≈≈

Then I started hearing a voice.

"Next time you and Rachel get into a fight, stop and give her a hug," it said after a particularly bad fight with my stepdaughter.

The advice was reasonable. Rachel was hurting after her mother walked out on her life. *Why not?* I knew the same pain of rejection.

The opportunity came the next afternoon. I reached out for an awkward hug. She pulled back, then finally relaxed in my embrace. A long road loomed ahead, but we'd taken the first step.

My fears continued to assault me.

"Reconcile with your father," came the same voice.

Is he dying? What do I say?

"Write a letter," came the reply. "I'll tell you what to say."

I hadn't talked to my father in years. I had no clue where to start, but the voice whispered words into my heart. Within minutes, I tucked my letter into an envelope and mailed it.

Days later, my father called. Tears welled up in my eyes as the walls came down.

ॐ ॐ ॐ

I took a long drag from my cigarette and slipped outside to enjoy the warm July evening. Maybe the voice would speak to me again. Another fight with my stepdaughter left me on edge.

Casey's puppy, Junie, trotted after me through the birch trees, my favorite place to escape. A grackle flew among the branches, while a songbird called to its mate.

"It's time to get going," the now familiar voice spoke aloud. "We have things to do."

I turned around, expecting the voice to reveal himself. The haze lifted, and I recognized Jesus.

It's you.

Jesus smiled.

Until now, I'd never paired the voice with the gentle man who'd been reaching out his arms. I'd been searching for rescue in all the wrong places. Jesus had been there all along.

I hurried inside and found a Bible in the back of a bookcase. Jesus spoke to me, his words pouring off the page like water to satisfy my thirst. I read for hours. I couldn't stop.

I read about a woman caught in adultery. I knew the same shame, yet Jesus told her accusers, "Let him who is without sin among you be the first to throw a stone" (John 8:7b ESV). His unconditional love flowed over me, drenching me from my toes to my every strand of hair. My Savior came not to condemn — but to rescue me. My love for him swelled inside me.

He held out his arms.

And I walked into his embrace.

His voice spoke even louder through the Bible. Everywhere I looked, a new lesson awaited.

Jesus talked to me about my fears.

"Why are you holding onto your fear?"

I didn't know how to answer, so he lifted my chin. "I didn't give you a spirit of timidity, but a spirit of power, of love and of self-discipline."

I walked out into the dark and repeated the words over and over until I believed the message.

Within days, my husband and the kids noticed the change in me.

"What happened to you?" Justin asked. "It's like you did a 180."

"I know." I couldn't quit grinning. "Isn't it great?" I told him about Jesus.

Justin admitted praying to Jesus as a kid, but choosing a different path as an adult.

I couldn't believe it. The deepest peace and joy flooded my life. My years in the occult never empowered me with the real transforming power I now found in Jesus.

"Instead of your shame," Jesus said through his words in Isaiah 61, "you will receive a double portion, and instead of disgrace you will rejoice in your inheritance … For he has clothed me with garments of salvation and arrayed me in a robe of his righteousness."

જાજાજા

My hunger eventually led me to Northgate Alaska Church. Not only did I continue to learn more about God, I started to grow in community with others. The pastors encouraged me to use the gifts God had given me to help others. SOZO, a ministry based on the Greek word meaning "saved, healed and delivered," was particularly precious to me. I began to see my real value. God could use my gifts and my pain as an opportunity to point others to the same freedom I had found.

After seeing *Nefarious*, a documentary on sex trafficking, my heart was stirred for the girls caught in modern-day slavery. Their faces burned on my mind; I knew the same feeling of being trapped. With the high rate of homeless teens in the Valley, I had to do something, so I joined three other women from Northgate. Today, we are working toward getting a shelter in the Valley for women and at-risk youth. We are also working toward opening a chapter of Kingdom Kids, a camp ministry for foster kids, a group especially vulnerable to sex trafficking. I'm excited to see what God will do. I stand in awe of his great love. I'm living proof that I am not the person I was. There is hope in Jesus. Just like I found.

ॐॐॐ

"Be real. Be vulnerable. Be authentic," Jesus recently repeated the message until I responded.
How, Lord?
"Share your story."
The next Sunday, Pastor Phil passed out a survey at church.
My heart skipped a beat. I knew exactly what Jesus wanted. I filled out the survey, and a writer called me.

"Where do you want to start your story?" she asked.

I thought for a moment and then began.

Small orbs of light danced around the room. They spiraled and dipped, flitting through the air like fireflies on a midsummer night.

I gazed at their sparkly reflection in my grandmother's ornate mirror while she plaited my long blond hair. My parents had left for work before I'd awoken.

"Liebchen." Her thick German broke my trance. "What are you dreaming about ... "

BRINGING BREATH TO BONES
THE STORY OF MONICA
WRITTEN BY ALLISON PITTMAN

My hand shook as I dialed, causing me to try again and again, even though the number was familiar. More than familiar, in fact. It was my own — the telephone number of our family's house in my home country — the one I shared with my husband and our three children whenever our work didn't require me to be in the apartment we kept in Alaska. I couldn't explain my trepidation, other than some instinctive, deep-seated fear.

I heard the phone ring once. Twice. It was late, but not so late that my husband, Dimitri, wouldn't be awake, so I was surprised when the small, shaky voice of my daughter, Sasha, came into my ear.

"Hello?"

"Sasha, darling. It's Mom." A bit of silence threatened to twist my stomach, but I soldiered on, forcing a bit of normalcy to my voice. It had been nearly three weeks since I'd seen my husband. The duties of our work often required me to travel to Alaska while Dimitri stayed home in our native country. Our marriage lived on separate continents, but tonight the distance seemed greater than ever. "Can you put Dad on the phone? I just have a quick question about some paperwork."

Now, the silence stretched, like one of those old-fashioned phone cords, and I found my fist clenched on itself. Long before I heard the words, I knew what my daughter was going to say.

"He's not here, Mom."

I looked at the clock and bit my lip. Almost midnight.

"Do you know where he is? Did he say when he'd be back?"

"He's not coming back tonight." A long pause. "He's at that woman's house."

I gripped the phone tighter, if only to keep myself from throwing it across the room. Sadly, my husband's infidelities were nothing new. He'd done little to hide his adultery from me, the children or even our small community. But there was something about this moment, this betrayal — maybe it was that small, embarrassed tone in my daughter's voice, forced to report her father's conduct. Fighting back tears, I told Sasha I loved her, hung up the phone and fell to my knees.

Where had I gone wrong?

My very blood seemed to have turned to ice within me, and I remained cold and alone. Years of pain had chipped my flesh away, and at that moment I was no longer Monica, faithful wife of a vibrant evangelist.

"Monica," he'd said, not long after our first date. "I've asked God to bring me a woman who will love me unconditionally. Someone who can share my vision, who will support me, no matter where life takes us."

It was as if he'd written our vows before he even

proposed. And then, my husband, for all his public Christianity, had turned our marriage into an endless lie. I reached up to the couch, found a pillow and, still on the floor, curled myself around it.

"Oh, God," I whispered, searching for the familiar comfort of prayer. My very bones ached against the hardness of the floor. It wasn't the first time I'd been betrayed by a man I trusted to protect me. I felt small, and as I closed my eyes, I was transported to the time and place where the pain began …

෨෨෨

I was 12 years old, and the only sound in our apartment was the scratching of my pencil on the paper as I worked through a complex math equation. Mama wasn't there to help, of course. She'd be at work until 6 p.m. As the only one of her siblings to escape the poverty of her small village and get a degree in engineering, Mama had little patience for anyone with an inability to understand what she calls "simple" algebra.

I looked at the clock and calculated. Two hours until Mama would get home. There was still an hour's worth of homework, at least. Then chores, preparing supper, running the sweeper over the carpets. Dusting our well-worn furniture. Never enough time to get everything done, but if I didn't, Mama might fly into one of her rages. I needed to hurry, before —

"Monica."

Oh, no. The voice came from the bedroom Mama shared with Michael, my stepfather. The only father I'd ever known, really. He was the reason I hated those afternoons, the unending stretch of time alone. Or, almost alone.

Ever since I was 6 years old, he'd made our house a place of torment. I'd told Mom, of course, way back when it started, when I was too young to really understand what he was doing to me. But she didn't believe me. Rather, she believed him more, especially when he said that I — a child — had somehow invited his attention. But he'd promised to be better, and I guess he was, for a while. For four years, at least. But it started again when I turned 10, and since Mom hadn't believed me the first time, there seemed no reason to tell her now.

His voice was thick with persistence. "You out there, sweetheart?"

I could tell he'd been drinking, and I immediately began to anticipate the smell and the taste of liquor. For a moment, like always, I thought maybe, if I remained perfectly still, he wouldn't know I was there. He'd think I'd gone to a friend's house to study or that I had dance class after school. Over in the corner Mama's dress form was draped with a half-finished costume for an upcoming competition. In that, at least, I felt Mama's love.

"Monica."

My pencil lead broke on a half-written numeral, because I realized there was no longer a closed door between us. I didn't have to turn around to see him. I knew his face would be grizzled from a long day's sleep, and I knew his breath and skin would reek with the beer and whiskey he consumed throughout every waking hour. His voice reached out and landed on the back of my neck, just as his first touch had when I was 6 years old.

"Get in here," he said. And with sickness rising within me, I obeyed.

☙ ☙ ☙

It had taken me a lifetime to forget the shame of my stepfather's touch, but on that night it resurfaced, buoyed by the familiar pain of betrayal. When my stepfather married my mother, he should have taken on the responsibility of protecting me, just as Dimitri had promised to love, honor and cherish me. My stepfather hurt me long before I even fully understood the nature of my pain. In the beginning, Dimitri's infidelity was confusing, too.

I remember one afternoon, early in our marriage, when we were both studying at Bible college, we were just sitting, side-by-side, working on some paper or another while the children — we had two by then — played quietly in the corner. All of a sudden, I felt his eyes on me, and I looked up, curious.

"You know," he said, as if we'd been in the middle of a conversation, "we live in such a big city. You would never know if I cheated on you."

I thought it was some kind of joke, and I remember

smiling and saying, "Why? Are you planning to?"

He didn't smile back. "Just an observation," he said and returned to his work.

At the time, I'd thought it a strange thing to say, but brushed it off as an odd observation. Nothing more. But then he took advantage of my trust, and just as my mother doubted my initial accusations, I knew the world would never believe that Dimitri is capable of such emotional cruelty. So all this time I'd kept it quiet, to myself.

"It isn't supposed to be like this," I said, speaking out to God from my place on the floor. I wasn't curled around my pillow anymore, but sitting up, my back against the sofa, legs splayed out in front of me in complete disregard for how rumpled my skirt would be. "I married a Christian man. That was supposed to solve everything. Not like the first time …"

کی کی کی

For most of my teenage years, life at home with my mother and stepfather could only be described as a living hell. I craved a safe home and a loving mother, and when I met Arik, I found both. He was more than a boyfriend; we became like a family as his mother welcomed me into their family. By the time I was 16, we were a family in every way, and I had a baby to anchor me there. It was wonderful when we were all together, but the time came to grow up and move out.

One evening, I was 18 years old, and my daughter was

fast asleep in the makeshift crib in the corner of our tiny one-room apartment.

"Sweet Sasha," I said, touching her face. My hand still bears a scar from long ago, when my mother's rage erupted in a dish thrown across the room, and I'd cut myself trying desperately to please her by cleaning it up. At that moment the scar rested against my baby's warm, soft cheek, and I felt a sense of hope, a promise for the future and a fierce need to protect her from harm.

I heard the sound of the door opening behind me, and I turned to see the shadow of Arik, my first husband, outlined by the hallway light.

"Shhh," I said, holding a finger to my lips. I got up and crossed the room to be wrapped in his arms. Instantly, I felt safe. In fact, Arik had been making me feel just this way since I was about 15 years old when I'd tried to put together some sort of normal life for myself. Part of that normalcy included an escape from my own home, and Arik's had been my refuge. I'd spent hours there, with him and his mother, marveling at the unfamiliar warmth of family and the ease with which the two lived. I suppose I loved Arik as a boyfriend, but I hungered for a family. So, when I found myself pregnant at 16, I was thrilled. It seemed an escape at first. Fun, even. But life is hard on a young marriage, and each day, that became more and more clear.

I lifted my head up for a kiss and tasted liquor, but I ignored it and pressed on with the question I'd been waiting all evening to ask.

"Did you get the job?"

"I don't want to talk about it." He kissed the top of my head.

I buried my face in his shirt, smelling the grease and the smoke of the bar where I knew he'd spent most of the day, and while I knew it would dispel the peace of this moment, I pressed on.

"We have to talk about it, Arik. We need milk for the baby, and the rent — the landlord won't give us another extension."

Angry, he pushed me away. "Can't you even wait until I get through the door?"

"I'm sorry," I said, trying to apologize with a second embrace, but he was already standing in front of our little refrigerator. There wasn't much in there besides bread, cheese and beer, and the bottles rattled against each other when he slammed the door.

"You've got to get off my back," he said after a long drink. "I just got out of the Army three months ago. It takes time."

Instinctively, I stood between him and the baby, though he'd never displayed even a hint of harm. "I didn't mean —"

"I don't think this is going to work."

"You don't mean that." I wrested the beer bottle away from him and took a long drink myself, hoping it would settle my heart. Our home was small and shabby, furnished with castoffs from his mother's attic and things rescued from back alley boxes, but it was ours. It was *mine.* And if my husband left, I'd never be able to pay the rent on my own. And if I left — "Where would I go?"

He shrugged. "Your mother's?"

❧ ❧ ❧

I did move back in with my mother. But, of course, I was still a child then, even with a child of my own, and Mama's house was safe, with my stepfather finally locked up for his crimes against me. As brief as my marriage to Arik was, it taught me the value of family. Simple, sweet togetherness. I guess that's why I stayed silent for as long as I did. My complaining had driven Arik away. I didn't want to lose a second husband.

And so, when Dimitri decided to become a minister, I went along with him.

"I believe I've been given authority to bring Christ to the people," he'd said.

There was no denying the passion in his voice. It was a passion I'd never heard any time he spoke to me.

"That's asking a lot of our family," I said, treading carefully lest I sound like I was complaining. "We have three children now, and to have to depend on the generosity of strangers to take care of them —"

"Where is your faith?" he asked.

"In Jesus," I said, but when it was clear that answer didn't suffice, I added, "And you."

I meant it at the time, too. God always met our needs, even when we were forced to make our home on the basement floor of generous friends. And even when he started drinking — just like my stepfather, just like Arik — I didn't complain, even though I knew it could lead to trouble. And when I knew Dimitri was sleeping with other women — well, for some reason it was enough that he wanted me to be his wife.

More than that, I thought God wanted me to be his wife, wanted me to follow him, because long before I met Dimitri, I'd decided to follow Jesus. And I followed Jesus because I followed a boy ...

∽∽∽

We'd been living at Mama's for almost three years, Sasha and I, almost more like sisters than mother and daughter. Those days, living with Mama, I felt more like a kid than I ever did growing up. Maybe it's because my stepfather was in prison or because in her role as a grandmother, Mama wasn't acting like such a bully anymore. Maybe it was because Sasha was the most beautiful little girl in the world, and she filled the whole place with joy.

One day, when I was 21 years old, I was zipping up a new pair of blue jeans, turning to and fro, studying myself in the full-length mirror. I looked happy, healthy and strong, but inside, I knew something was missing. American rock-and-roll music blared on the radio, and Sasha was dancing. I joined her, singing the lyrics into my hairbrush.

Jeans zipped, lipstick on, I turned to my 5-year-old daughter and asked, "What do you think?"

"Pretty!" She clapped her little hands enthusiastically, and I swooped her up in a hug.

I had a date that night, like I did most nights, though I'd never introduced any of my boyfriends to my daughter. There'd never been anything serious, and I knew well the dangers of bringing a man into the house. I wanted to protect her from everything — even from myself. I didn't think she'd love me as much if she knew what happened when I walked out the door. The drinking, the parties and, yes, the boyfriends that she'd never know. Somewhere, deep down, I harbored a hope of finding the perfect man, someone who would love both me and her, keeping us safe and protected forever.

I kissed her goodbye, told Mama I was leaving and walked out into the city.

In some ways, it seemed like all of my home country had become one thriving, vibrant teenager. The end of Communism opened us up to the rest of the world, and that went beyond blue jeans and music. We were wild, hungry for new ideas to fuel this new freedom.

Across the street, I saw my latest boyfriend, and I quickened my step to meet him. He was nothing like Arik. His name was Markus, and he carried this energy about him that I'd never felt before.

"Hi, Monica," he said, taking my hand and giving me a chaste kiss on the cheek. Unlike all the other guys, this is all he'd ever tried to do. He grinned, and a new light was introduced into my life. "How would you like to try something a little different this evening?"

"Like what?"

He looked nervous. "A new church."

Church. Along with music and fashion, it was something new to our lately liberated country. No longer restricted by the Atheism of the Communist regime, they were popping up everywhere, like bears coming out of hibernation. I hadn't paid too much attention, though. Every moment I wasn't spending with my daughter, I was living out my overdue adolescence. Now here this beautiful boy, one of the nicest I'd met since Sasha's father, wanted me to go to church with him?

"Sure." I'd go with him anywhere.

It was some kind of celebration, with food and music. They were gathered in a theater at a university, and I've never seen so many happy people in one place. It seemed a little strange to count myself as one of them, so I kept myself close to Markus' side, wondering why he would bring me there. If these people knew — if *he* knew — everything about my past ... what my stepfather had done to me, how I'd gotten pregnant when I was just 16, that I was already a divorced woman with a kid. They were singing songs about Jesus, songs about how much they loved him and how much he loves us. Everybody looked so ... clean. Inside and out. And I felt like I had some kind of dark, oppressive film covering every inch of my body.

Markus, though, was perfect. He introduced me to all of his friends, and they smiled and embraced me as if I'd always been a part of them, and soon I was swept up in it, too. I didn't know the words to any of the songs, but I raised my hands along with everybody else. My head was so jumbled with questions I could hardly hear what the preacher was saying, and what I did hear I didn't quite understand. At some point he — the preacher — held his arms out to the audience. Calling to us, beckoning us. I felt unbalanced, and it took only the slightest nudge from Markus to send me out into the aisle, walking to the front with the sounds of voices singing all around me. I was not alone. Others had walked to the front, too, and I saw them there, down on their knees, so I joined them.

It felt almost like a war raged above my head, but inside I felt nothing but this powerful, warm, strong pressure trying to fight its way out. I heard the people around me praying, and I wanted to pray, too, but words wouldn't come out. I didn't know what to say. How could I? Still, I felt a change within me. Like an ugliness pouring out of me. Everything that I hated about myself shrank away, making room for this new presence. At that moment, I recognized the combatants in the war raging around me. It was Jesus, who had been nothing to me all my life, fighting against every man who had ever caused me pain. Jesus battling the father who abandoned me, the stepfather who molested me for eight years, the husband who didn't love me enough and the string of boyfriends who didn't love me at all. And with the silent flow of my tears, Jesus conquered them all. The heat inside of my body was replaced with a calm, cooling sense of victory.

Then, slowly, one-by-one, my voice joined the others, with a simple prayer. Not for myself, because I knew already that I had somehow become powerful, victorious. Instead, the first words that came out of my mouth were the ones I wish someone had prayed for me.

"Jesus, save my child."

Later, in the quiet darkness of the night, I knelt beside my daughter's bed, and I waited to see if everything I felt at the church earlier that day was still within me, and it was. I felt only peace and hope, but I knew if I was going to be strong enough for my daughter, I couldn't just ask for Jesus to save her. He had to save me first. I held her hand and whispered a prayer, this time the words flowing out like sweet spring rain.

"Jesus, thank you for saving me."

๛๛๛

At dawn the morning after my long-distance call home, I woke up dreaming about that boy, Markus, wondering what would have happened if I had married him. But we were young, and within a few months, I was crying into my cookies and tea, mourning the fact that he'd gone on to love another. As would I, when I met the enigmatic, irresistible Dimitri, ready to rescue me from heartache.

The phone rang, interrupting the morning's stillness. By the number I could see that it was him, home from his night with his mistress, probably full of the same false remorse I'd seen too many times before. The phone rang and rang, but I ignored its plea for attention.

Eventually, it rang long enough for the answering machine to pick up, and I heard him.

"Monica, darling. I know you're there. I know you're listening, but you must understand. I —"

It was the last I heard before hitting the mute button. I didn't want another apology. I didn't need an explanation. How had we gone from that vibrant, loving couple, to this? He in bed with another woman. Me miles away, on top of the covers, fully dressed, alone. In some ways, I guess, he is still the charismatic young man able to sweep people into church and women into his arms. And for so long, I've been willing to be a part of that, suffering in silence. Smiling through pain. I've prayed for Jesus to turn the heart of my husband back to me. I've prayed for our family to be whole and healthy.

But there was nothing healthy about this. I felt used up. Dried up. Nothing but bones. I'd fled to Arik's house to escape my stepfather. I'd run into Markus' arms to escape a life of sin. I'd trusted Dimitri to make me into the good Christian woman I so longed to be. And now? Where was there to go?

My Bible sat beside me on the bed. I rested my hand upon it, listlessly running my thumb across the pages. I'd slept little, and the dreams of my former full, carefree spirit gave way to the reality of my present state, bringing to mind a memory of a favorite scripture from the book of Ezekiel. The Spirit of the Lord took Ezekiel out to a valley full of bones and led him to walk back and forth among them, until the Lord asked, "Son of man, can these bones live?"

My night of reflection had been a journey through a valley of bones. In my heart I heard God asking me a similar question. *Monica, can you live?*

I spoke out into the gray morning light.

"Oh, Lord. You alone know."

I stood, slowly, and smoothed the clothing I'd been wearing since the day before. Feeling like I might snap with every step, I found the strength to go into the kitchen and make a cup of tea. Then, as had long been my habit, I sat at the table and opened my Bible to the passage.

Ezekiel, chapter 37, verses 5-6: "This is what the Sovereign Lord says to these bones. I will make breath enter you, and you will come to life. I will attach tendons to you and make flesh come upon you and cover you with skin; I will put breath in you, and you will come to life. Then you will know that I am the Lord."

For so long, I'd been depending on my husband to breathe life into me. I'd tied my life with Jesus to my life with Dimitri, living with the alcohol and the adultery without question. And what had it brought me? I had nothing else to give — not to my children, not to myself and not even to my Lord. I needed strength, but that strength would have to come from God himself. For the first time, I would have to fully rely on him to be my heavenly father and provider.

"I have to leave him."

I spoke the words aloud, surprised at the strength behind them. Still, shame tempted me. What would everybody think? What would they say? Another failed marriage. A woman not good enough to keep her husband. The years of dysfunction heaped upon my children.

But then, a promise. Long before I had a Bible, I had a small book of God's promises — verses pulled from scripture, arranged topically, meant to bring the reader directly into the understanding of the life God wants for his children. In my first years as a Christian, I'd sat at our family table, my mother at work and Sasha playing in the background, while Mrs. Palek, a lovely older neighbor lady, read through this promise book with me. I had a favorite promise back then, one perfectly crafted for a 21-year-old single mother with a life nearly ruined by abuse and sin. Now, I found it in my Bible, and the words were as powerful that morning as they ever were. Isaiah 50:7: "Because the Sovereign LORD helps me, I will not be disgraced. Therefore have I set my face like flint, and I know I will not be put to shame."

Flint. Necessary to the production of fire, and just as I'd felt a burning when I first prayed to God to forgive me of my sins, I felt that burning again. Not a burning of shame, but a flame of peace. The phone rang again, but this time, armed with the strength of God's promise, I answered.

UNBREAKABLE KINDNESS
The Story of Peter
Written by Douglas Abbott

"You can kiss me goodbye!" I told my best friend, James. "I'm going to jail for a long time."

James said nothing. His eyes were murky with fear.

We were standing in the snow, watching a police officer search the cab of my truck. The vehicle's headlamps were throwing great cones of light over us. It felt as though the harsh beams were laying open the contents of my soul. I couldn't believe this was happening.

I knew I would be taken into custody as soon as the officer discovered the ounce of marijuana sitting in plain sight on the back seat, or the pipes and scale in the glove box, or the sawed-off shotgun in the duffel bag behind the driver's seat. Even if he missed all that, there was a mirror covered with cocaine sitting underneath the driver's seat. There was no way out of this.

I could hear prison doors slamming shut. I imagined myself marching through chow lines in a fluorescent-orange jumpsuit. It would be a long time before I breathed free air again.

James and I stood frozen, waiting for disaster to fall. Splashes of red and blue from the cop's flashers swirled on the snow. My mind was spinning. What had possessed me to behave so recklessly? Suddenly I saw the truth with awful clarity: I lived in chains. I had traded my future away for daily installments of drug-induced euphoria. I was beaten. And now I was going to jail. Foul images from Hollywood prison films came to mind.

The cop emerged from the truck and turned toward us. His posture was strangely casual.

"Okay, everything looks all right here. But you can't park here. You'll have to clear out."

James and I exchanged looks, trying not to let the officer see the amazement and relief we were feeling. Was this cop completely blind?

We didn't need a second invitation. We left quickly, hooting with joy the second we exited the cul-de-sac. I reflected later how a person's mental clarity can evaporate the moment critical pressure is lifted.

Just seconds before, standing like a deer in my own headlights, I had seen my foolishness — the savagery of my own addiction to drugs — and wished fervently that I had made different choices. Now it was as though none of it had ever happened.

"James, reach between my legs and fish that mirror out from under my seat."

He hesitated. "I don't want to pull that thing out right here. Let's wait till we get where we're going."

"Do you want to lose our party going over a pothole? Just do it!"

James did as he was told. "Whatever you do, don't move your legs."

As soon as he had tidied everything up, James swore softly and shook his head. "I can't believe that cop let us go."

I nodded. "Me, either. It doesn't make any sense. Do you think he was just cutting us a break?"

"Why would he do that? He made a pretty big production of having us get out of the truck and stand in the headlights. Why would he pretend to search the truck if he was just planning to let us go?"

I shrugged. "I don't know." I assumed a mock-serious expression. "But what I do know is that he did the right thing. Finally, justice and common sense are beginning to prevail on the streets. That man should receive a medal!"

James brayed laughter. "Amen, brother!"

We went on our way, laughing and carrying on as though we hadn't both come within an inch of disaster.

However, I could no longer ignore my brush with long-term incarceration. It was too clear an indicator of the degree to which my drug use was altering my life. It seemed obvious that, sooner or later, my compulsions would land me right back in this kind of situation — or worse. Then there was the deeper question of exactly what had happened that night. It simply wasn't possible that the cop could have missed all the contraband in my truck. And yet he had. What could possibly account for it?

The questions didn't have any reasonable answers. And no matter what answers I went with, I couldn't dismiss the crisis that had swept into my life. Change was coming. Through the soul-searching that ensued over the following weeks, the evening's brush with the law would prove to be a pivotal event that would change the entire course of my life.

❧❧❧

I wasn't abused as a child. I had loving, supportive parents and a stable upbringing. I was given everything a child needs to be healthy and whole. The truth is that there is almost no limit to the number of ways people can go wrong.

My affinity for chemical intoxication began when I was in the fifth grade. My parents were hosting a gathering with friends and put us to bed early. I expressed my anger by stealing alcohol from the cabinet. I drank until I puked and passed out. It was an early example of what would become for me a pattern of extreme self-indulgence and excess.

I wish I had taken a hint from the experience. However, I was quick to learn that rebellion brought rewards — in particular, more attention from my parents. So I took to fighting with my mother over minuscule house policies.

One day I asked if I could go Rollerblading with my friends.

"You know better than that," my mom said patiently. "You can't go anywhere until you've finished your social studies report."

I hadn't expected her to remember about the report.

"Why do I have to do it today? I have all weekend to get it done."

My mother ignored my petulant tone. "Or you have all weekend to skate, just as soon as you get your homework done," she said with a winsome smile. "See how that works? Get your obligations out of the way, and you can enjoy yourself. Best of all, you won't walk into class without your homework."

"I don't care about my homework. School is a grown-up's invention for tormenting kids." I walked off without waiting for a response.

The next day, I approached her as she sat at the kitchen table and handed her the report.

"Now can I go Rollerblading?" I asked with a bit of exasperation.

She looked at me over her reading glasses. "No, because now your room is a disaster. Peter, you are perfectly aware of the rules. Do you really expect me to waive them just because you want something? Why don't you try policing yourself? Then we won't have to go through this all the time. Now please go and clean your room, and then you can do all the Rollerblading you want."

That was the day I decided to run away. That afternoon, while making marginal progress on my room, I gathered a haphazard assortment of supplies. That night, as soon as the house was quiet, I lowered a suitcase to the ground from my bedroom window with a rope and then climbed down after it. I treaded delicately through our backyard, climbed over the fence and ascended the hill toward the highway.

My friend Forrest didn't know what to think when I rapped on his bedroom window.

He rolled out of bed, rubbing sleep out of his eyes with the heels of his hands. He walked to the window and opened it a crack.

"What are you doing?" he asked incredulously. "You're going to get me in trouble."

"I'm running away," I told him. "I need your help."

"How am I supposed to help you? Don't be stupid."

I just stood there until Forrest relented and dug up some canned fish, a map and a flashlight. "This is all I can give you," he said. "Now go, before my parents wake up."

I proceeded on, following the highway, which ran along fields and patches of spruce and birch. My plan was to stay with my grade-school girlfriend, Amanda, and it was a long hike to her house. I stopped several times to rest along the way.

Just after first light, as I was walking along, a car pulled to the side of the road up ahead. It was my parents. I stopped and set my suitcase down. My mom got out on the passenger side and stood there without a word. For some reason, I just got in the car quietly.

My parents didn't punish me. After they had brought me home, they sat me down in the living room. My mom did most of the talking.

"Peter, we're not angry. But we wouldn't be very good parents if we didn't address this. You can't just go running off whenever you're unhappy. Your father and I want you to come to us when something's bothering you."

I said nothing. All of a sudden, my grievances seemed silly.

"We discussed the possibility of flying you to Washington to live with your aunt and uncle. Do you think you'd be happier there?"

Whether it was reverse psychology or a straightforward offer, the answer was no.

I knew perfectly well I didn't want to go and live with Uncle Charlie and Aunt Sue. They would probably be much stricter than my parents. Without question, such an arrangement would mean a sharp decline in my standard of living. I had it a whole lot better than I'd thought just a few hours ago.

"No, Mom. I shouldn't have run away. I'm sorry. I want to stay here."

And that was that. My parents had used reason to deflate my hopes of escaping their rules. There would be no more impromptu misadventures. There would be no more running away.

༂༂༂

My father was a man of few words. His convictions about the importance of honesty, integrity and moral conduct were displayed in his actions. He was stoic and uncompromising about providing for his family. He possessed a natural strength of character that had enabled him to dodge drug addiction, irresponsibility and other pitfalls of youth.

When I was in middle school, my dad took a job as an oilfield worker in Prudhoe Bay, Alaska. The work kept him away two weeks out of each month. His regular absence gave me an unprecedented level of personal freedom, which I used to indulge my growing fondness for alcohol, marijuana and pornography. Without any awareness on my part, the substance abuse began to eclipse everything else in my life, including my long-term perspective. I had no inkling that these easy pursuits were an impediment to my goals of attending college and becoming a rich, successful attorney.

I approached high school as an opportunity for unlimited debauchery. Ironically, my access to drugs was never greater than during my four years of high school. Getting high did not prevent me from excelling in my courses, as well as in sports. Furthermore, my increasing involvement with substances gave me desirable sway in social circles. I lived the dream of every freshman: girls, popularity and respect. My life was a perpetual party. I had added into the mix some dangerous elements: cocaine, crack and psychedelic drugs. I also discovered that by selling drugs I could manage the impossible logistics of personal supply.

Even as my life was lurching off the tracks, I was the all-American picture of success. During my senior year, I made All-State in football and became both homecoming king and prom king. Meanwhile, I had the comfortable backing of my family's upper-middle-class lifestyle. I can only imagine how my peers would have reacted to the knowledge that inside the student leader and football star they so admired was a train wreck of misery and insecurity. I fully expected to die of a drug overdose. I made jokes about how they would make an afterschool special movie about me after finding my bloated corpse. I used perverse humor to blunt the truth that my love of chemical euphoria and life's cheap pleasures had undermined the wealth of academic and social opportunities being offered to me.

෨෨෨

During my senior year, the consequences of my self-made empire of hedonism started to catch up with me. One day, I was approached during lunch break by a girl I had dated casually a few times. Stacey came up to me with a wan look on her face.

"Peter, we need to talk."

I was discussing football with my teammates. "Sure. How about after school? I have a short day today."

"We really should talk now."

"Okay. Talk."

"Somewhere else."

We went outside and walked around the track. We found ourselves sharing the area with a few dedicated souls running laps and jumping hurdles. We kept close to the bleachers.

"You look nice," I said, trying to make conversation. The truth was that I was beginning to get nervous. Stacey was being way too serious.

She looked up at me. "I'm pregnant."

I stopped walking and turned toward her. "What did you say?"

She stopped to keep even with me. "I'm pregnant," she said simply.

"If this is a joke, it's not funny."

She just kept looking up at me.

This was the worst thing she could have told me. It took me a minute to find my tongue. "How did that happen?"

A look of disgust crossed her features.

"Perhaps you remember the evenings we spent in your truck. You insisted on continuing to put your hand under my skirt —"

"What? Don't blame me for this. You were supposed to be on the pill."

"I *was* on the pill. It's not infallible, remember?"

I said nothing for a minute. We kept walking along the track. I could hear wheezing and the thuds of shoes hitting the pavement. I wished I were running laps instead of having this conversation.

I rubbed my face and heard a strange guttural noise that I realized was me, groaning. "Oh, my God, Stacey. I can't believe this is happening."

I looked over at Stacey. She was beginning to cry. Her face was contorted with pain. I had to look away.

"You can't believe this is happening?" she mimicked. Her voice was filled with indignation and distorted because of her tears. "Peter, we have a child together."

"*Wait* a minute. You're not actually thinking of having the baby, are you?"

Stacey stopped walking and looked full into my face. Her mouth gaped open with shock. Then she started crying full-bore, her face in her hands.

"Look, I'm sorry," I said lamely. "I'm not ready for this. Is it my fault that the pill didn't take?"

Stacey dropped her hands and looked at me. Her face was wet. "Your *fault?*" She was angry now. Her voice was tremulous with emotion. "Do you even have a soul? I can't *believe* you!" And she turned and ran from the track.

At the moment, I felt nothing but anger and revulsion. I wanted no part of fatherhood. I didn't even have the illusion of love for this young woman. I did not permit myself to consider the pain Stacey had to be going through. In my unruly self-indulgence, all I could see was how the fallout would place limitations on my freedom.

My expeditious response to this unwelcome development during every conversation afterward was to pressure Stacey to have an abortion, which I told her was the only option I would consider.

"What if I have the baby anyway?" she asked, more than once.

"Well, then, you're on your own. I'm not going to throw my football career away because some lousy pill didn't work."

So Stacey consented to the abortion.

A week after the pregnancy was discovered, I was confronted angrily by her mother, Melinda, who was a substitute teacher at our school. She had observed me cavorting amorously with a different girl just as her daughter's condition was coming to light. She approached me at the school.

"My daughter is suffering because of you," she said with steel in her voice. "You're walking around here with your next squeeze like nothing happened. Let me tell you something: You're going to suffer, too. I'm going to call your mother and tell her about the whole thing."

I had been hoping to conceal this from my mom. She wouldn't take the news well, much less my desire to pressure Stacey into getting an abortion. When I pulled into the driveway at home, my father shot me a look from inside the garage. I climbed out of the car, and he met me at the top of the driveway.

"Your mother's pretty upset," he said heavily. "You'd better go in and talk to her."

I actually considered simply leaving, so much was I dreading the confrontation with my mom. We had a close relationship, and I knew she had strong moral convictions. And in the end, she was a *woman*. It would be almost impossible for her not to be personally hurt by my actions. Stacey's pregnancy was blowing open the carefully concealed double life I had been living. This was a miserable development.

I plodded into the kitchen. My mom was standing at

the sink with the water running. She heard me come in and turned toward me. There was an incredible sadness in her eyes. She was weeping.

"You don't have to do this," she said to me, after we had limped awkwardly into the conversation.

"Mom, I don't want to have this child."

"There are other options —"

"I know, adoption, right? Which would leave some poor bastard child floating around out there with my DNA inside him."

"I'll raise the child. How about that?"

"Mom, don't you see? That would be even worse."

"Worse than killing it? Do you hear what you're saying? Please don't do this."

I was speechless. I knew my mother was right, but I felt as though I couldn't turn back.

"Stacey and I have made up our minds." There. I had said it.

"Well, I'm not going to be a part of it. Don't ask to borrow the money from us." And she turned back toward the sink.

On a grimy day, Stacey's mother drove us out to the clinic. Stacey was visibly troubled, occasionally crying. Melinda had the radio playing during the drive, and I used the afternoon news report to ignore the prickly tension of the situation in the car. The momentous item of the day was the forthcoming verdict in the O.J. Simpson trial. As we sat in the parking lot of the clinic in Melinda's pickup truck, we waited for the announcement: Not Guilty. I ruminated that even animals in Antarctica must be aware of this well-publicized farce. The news story would serve as a bizarre index to mark the day in my memory.

Melinda and I sat in the waiting room while Stacey went in to have the procedure. Not long after she had gone in, Melinda spoke. "Stacey's going to be fine."

I said nothing. I detected an undertone of contempt in her voice, as though she had wanted to add, "but *you* won't."

I believe she said it for her own benefit, but the comment managed to pierce my composure just the same. I knew the abortion was wrong, but in my self-absorption, I was resolved to go through with it if it killed me.

There was more turbulence the following April. Out of the blue, I was contacted and asked to come down to the police station. I walked in and found both my parents already seated with police detectives. They looked up at me somberly as I entered the room.

One of the detectives, a burly man in a plaid suit, began without preamble: "Peter, we need to know where you were on the evening of February 16th of this year."

I tried to act unconcerned. "I don't remember exactly. That was a couple of months ago."

"Were you in the Westchester neighborhood around that date?"

"I don't remember."

Then he came right out with it: "Did you break into the house on Orchard Street, Peter?" There was a hard light of knowledge in his eyes.

What the police already knew was that I and an accomplice had, in fact, committed a burglary there. We had been told there was a large harvest of marijuana plants to be had at the address. As it turned out, there were no plants there, but a surveillance camera had captured my image during the burglary, and the owner of the house had sent a copy of the video to the police. I discovered later that investigators had initially agreed to table the charges in deference to the school administrators' wishes so that I could finish out the wrestling season.

Now, however, wrestling was over, and reality caught up with me. I felt like an actor without a script. The detective bore down on me unflinchingly. I looked over at my parents. There was no help there, either. They both had looks on their faces that were at once disgusted and insistent. They fully expected me to confess to the crime.

"So what's it going to be, son?" the detective said.

I shook my head. "I told you, I didn't have anything to do with it."

The detective pulled a video cassette out of a drawer and slid it into a VCR on a cart against the wall. The television on top of the cart flickered to life. Grainy footage showed a door slamming open. Then I watched myself walk in and move through the house. I felt nauseous. There was no mistaking the identity of the people in the scene. The detective signaled to his cohort, who stopped the video. Then he just looked at me expectantly, his fingertips together, waiting for me to speak.

"Okay, you got me," I told him. "I did it." It felt inordinately phony to say the words. Of course I had done it. And now I had lost all the leverage I might have gained by confessing freely.

"Look, officer, I'm sorry for what I did. I wish I'd never done it."

There was a shadow of disdain in the cop's face. "I'll bet you do."

"Well, can I get some sort of consideration for making a confession?"

The detective reached into his desk and pulled out a legal pad and a pen. He put them on the desk in front of me. "Maybe. Write down the whole thing. Don't leave anything out. I'll tell the prosecutor that you confessed voluntarily. He may decide to cut you some slack."

Hence, I was formally charged with felony burglary. In spite of the hard exterior I presented to the police and the intake officer, I imagined the worst: jail, loss of my collegiate opportunities, life as a felon with a besmirched reputation. I realized also that, in addition to all this, my actions had affected my parents as well. We lived in a small town; everyone would find out about this. The benighted existence I had been living was catching up with me.

My case began to move through the criminal courts. I was 18 years old and was being prosecuted as an adult.

My parents made it clear to me that they had no desire to protect me from all the consequences of my stupidity.

"I have half a mind to let them nail you to the wall,"

my father said. "But I suspect you might learn a good lesson from this without blowing your schooling over it. I really don't want to see that happen."

"Neither do I," my mom agreed. "I can't imagine what you were thinking, Peter." She shook her head. "Well, there's nothing for it but to make the best of it. Don't expect us to step in if there should be a next time. You'll be on your own."

And so, thanks to the services of an attorney, my parents' lobbying on my behalf and some character references from the community, the judge granted a suspended imposition of sentence. That meant I would serve three years of probation, at the end of which, if I stayed out of trouble, the charges would be dropped.

The remainder of my senior year was a formality. I had earned all the credits I needed for graduation. My only scholastic concern had been to finish the wrestling season, which was now over. Meanwhile, I was hurtling into a blurry future. The pregnancy, the abortion and finally the skirmish with the law had scrubbed the blush of youth off me — without discouraging me from continuing my risky behaviors. I was marching into adulthood in a growing haze of chemical intoxication.

In spite of my drug-addled state, however, I was quite looking forward to college. First of all, it was an opportunity to see the world beyond the small town I had known all my life. I would be able to continue playing football, which I loved. There would be plenty of beautiful girls to meet. I would be out on my own. The unexpected outcome in the legal matter had salvaged everything for me, or so I thought.

❧❧❧

I traveled to the Western State University training camp in August 1996 and immediately began to feel intensely homesick. I didn't like Colorado or any of my new surroundings. I had unwittingly undergone a drastic reduction in stature by virtue of my membership in a class of superior athletes, most of whom possessed greater talents and physical characteristics than I had ever had. I was absolutely insignificant. I also discovered that I missed my girlfriend, Lisa. Furthermore, I was painfully conscious of being without my constant companion, marijuana, for which I had no immediate remedy. I had no friends or connections in Colorado — hence, no way to obtain the drug.

I returned home after only three weeks at the training camp. It was the latest in what had become a pattern of self-sabotage by which I would come right to the cusp of success only to withdraw. I felt a strange mixture of pain and relief — the latter because I was spared the uncertainty and discomfort of the entire venture. However, the impact of my failure was considerable. It was not merely a personal misstep. My parents had spent thousands of dollars to provide the opportunity I had discarded almost casually. The incident drove me deeper into the arms of my beloved substances and further out of relationships with friends and family. My life was completely stalled. But whatever thought I gave to changing, I did not for a moment think about getting clean. To the contrary, I used more than ever, as though, through sheer volume of consumption, I could resurrect the feeling of exhilaration my drug use had once produced for me.

Not long after my arrival back in Alaska, I moved out of my parents' house and began sharing quarters with my girlfriend, Lisa, and her father. There, I could smoke pot and drink beer without the smothering scrutiny I had endured at my parents' house. Lisa's father was easygoing, and my relationship with Lisa was somewhat turbulent but affectionate. Wages and tips from my pizza delivery job provided me with enough disposable income to stay loaded during my off hours.

ॐॐॐ

Not long after I moved in with Lisa, I underwent a tonsillectomy, following which I received strict orders not to smoke, since it might cause a breakage of the blood clot left from the surgery, which would in turn cause incessant bleeding.

The next night I completely disregarded the doctor's orders and spent an evening smoking crack cocaine with a friend David, who had made a half-hearted effort to talk me out of it.

"Man, I wouldn't be partying yet if I were you," he told

me when I showed up at his house. He knew all about the tonsillectomy, but he'd made the mistake of telling me his parents were gone for the evening, leaving the house free for us.

"Don't worry about it. I'll be fine," I said with a dismissive tone. "Call Mike."

He just gave me a "you're crazy" look and shook his head. Naturally, he wanted to party as much as I did.

We were smoking up a storm when it happened: After inhaling an enormous hit, I began coughing profusely. Blood sprayed out of my mouth, and I quickly realized that I had broken the blood clot.

David looked at me in horror. "Oh, my God, you're bleeding like crazy!" After a moment of fear-induced paralysis, he snatched up the phone to call the emergency room. His voice was two octaves higher than normal. "My friend is coughing and spraying blood all over the place!" he screamed into the receiver. "You have to help — no, he just had his tonsils out!"

Even after I stopped coughing, copious amounts of blood continued to flow into my mouth. I was terrified.

David slammed the handset back into the cradle. "We have to take you to the ER," he told me.

I shook my head. "No way. I can't go to the hospital."

David's eyes widened further. "Peter, the bleeding won't stop on its own. They just told me you're going to die if we don't get you in there! Now cut the crap and let's go. Now!"

I shook my head. "I guess I'm going to die, then.

There's no way I'm going to the emergency room." David just looked at me miserably.

I knew if I went to the hospital, my mom would find out that I had been smoking crack cocaine. She knew about the marijuana and the alcohol, but she had no idea about the rest. I pictured her face and knew I could never let her find out. Not about this.

I walked into the bathroom and looked into the mirror. I was 19 years old, and I was going to die. Standing there at the mirror, spitting mouthfuls of blood into the sink, I said out loud, "Help me." Immediately, I felt a warm presence all over my body. A feeling of peace enveloped me, and I knew I was going to live.

I stood there at the sink rinsing out my mouth, watching the color of the water go from dark red to light red, to pink and finally to clear. The bleeding had completely stopped.

❧ ❧ ❧

A few weeks later, I picked up my friend James for a night of merrymaking. We parked in a snowy cul-de-sac where no houses had yet been raised. It was a perfect spot to pursue our favorite pastime. We were generously supplied and started in with gusto as I poured several grams of cocaine onto a mirror. Then the flashing of police emergency lights filled the cabin of the truck with oscillating bursts.

My heart leapt in my chest. We were done. I told

James as much as we stood petrified outside the truck, squinting in the glare of the headlights, watching the cop search the cab of the vehicle. Even if it hadn't been sketchy enough for a pair of young men to be sitting parked in an empty cul-de-sac, I was on probation, which gave the police the right to search me for any reason. There would be no constitutional arguments about unlawful search and seizure, and there was enough contraband in my truck for a blind person to nail us. Moreover, since I was on felony probation and possessed a shotgun and a large quantity of cocaine, I might receive as much as 10 years in prison for this.

But miraculously, the cop finished and approached us with a bland expression on his face.

"Everything looks okay here, but you'll have to find another place to park."

James and I marveled at what had happened, but it would take a full week before I began to contemplate the deeper meaning of these recent events. There had been not just one, but two anomalies — utter aberrations — both in my favor. Each of them had occurred in a moment of extreme duress. One had been nothing less than a brush with death. The second, only marginally worse in my view, should by all rights have resulted in long-term incarceration for me. And yet, it appeared that a short prayer had altered the course of my life — *twice*.

৵৵৵

My mother had attempted to impart faith in God to me when I was a child. From childhood, I had believed in the Biblical account of Christ and known that, at the very least, I ought to be observing the Ten Commandments. However, my conviction had always been essentially an intellectual position that was easy enough for my personal desires to sweep aside. And so they had.

When I was 9 years old, I began to revolt against Christianity's stifling constraints by deliberately misbehaving in Sunday school, which embarrassed my mother enough so that she stopped requiring me to attend. This posture of rebellion against God became the basis of my entire self-centered philosophy of life, expressing itself in greater and greater dissolution as the years went on.

Up until the night I was bleeding over the sink, I hadn't prayed in years, hadn't once picked up my Bible. I had been making my own rules for 10 years. Now, a two-syllable utterance to God had brought an extravagant outpouring of good fortune to me. The twofold event — first the healing at the sink and then the apparent blinding of the police officer — had stood my entire theology on end. Here was the God whose commandments were etched in stone and enforced by torrents of burning sulfur from heaven, now coming instantly to my aid after I had ignored him for more than a decade of decadence and hubris. Who was this God who displayed kindness to creatures like me? What reason could he have for helping someone whose only motivation for acknowledging him after all these years was self-interest? Only love, greater and deeper than any I had ever imagined existed.

Over the next few weeks, that brief glimpse of God began to draw me in a whole new direction, like a deer catching a scent in the wind. Surely such a God as this would be the best friend I could ever have! I began reading my Bible and discussing everything I read with those I deemed credible and worthy of my trust.

I began to see that God's commands were an expression of his love. I discussed this with Maggie, a Christian friend of my mother's.

"Peter, God loves people too much to allow them to remain in darkness. If you had a little boy, how would you feel if he took to spending his time in a soot-filled basement, getting bitten by diseased rats and cutting himself on rusty nails in the dark? Wouldn't you want to get him out — even if he fought you for a while? And think of that same little boy, who might stay down there even after he was full grown, without a clue about the lovely things he could be enjoying up in the house — art, literature, music, sumptuous dinners around the table and the company of gracious people. This is what God wants to give you — things you haven't even seen yet. But it can only happen if you are willing to change. You saw something pretty remarkable that night you nearly bled to death, didn't you?"

"Yeah, I sure did!"

"That is the essence of God's heart toward us. He didn't come to shut you down, he came to help you! And you needed it! He wants to go to work in other areas of your life, too. He wants you to trust him enough to let him rearrange some things in your life. He wants it for your own good."

My selfish conduct and the wreckage it had produced in my life gave fresh urgency to scripture's imperatives. I read the Sermon on the Mount and felt a tug on my heart.

During one conversation with Maggie, I mentioned Lisa. Maggie realized from the context that the two of us were living together. She didn't say a word, but I saw something in her eyes that helped me gather the motivation to change. One Saturday evening not long afterward, I informed Lisa that the following day I was going to go to church, give my life to Christ and move out of the place we had been sharing.

The next morning, I met my mom in the parking lot of her church and told her of my intention to commit my life to Christ. She told me with tears on her cheeks how often she had prayed for this moment. As we stood there embracing, I wondered how I could have discounted this woman's loving instruction for so many years at such great cost — particularly now that I had seen the love she'd wanted me to know about — a love that seemed to stretch from the cosmos to help a stiff-necked rebel in his hour of need. This God was the guy I wanted on my side!

I went in to the service and found that I was riveted by the preacher's words. It felt as though every word he spoke was directed at me. The peace and overarching kindness I had sensed in God seemed to swell as I sat through the message that morning. The recent strange experiences, everything I had read in scripture and the conversations with Maggie all swirled in my head as I sat in the pew. Finally, the invitation was issued for anyone to come forward who was ready to publicly commit his or her life to Jesus, and I went forward, weeping as I went.

The following year contained for me both excitement and frustration. I read my Bible hungrily and sought out the company of Christian friends. I was not disappointed with the Christian life. I had been more than amply compensated for everything I had given up to approach God. I discovered that there was joy to be had in prayer, Bible study and other activities I had thought so boring and stifling before. I discovered that I had inherited a huge extended family in the members of my church.

However, I found that ridding myself of old habits — drinking to excess, drug use and promiscuity — wasn't as easy as simply acknowledging the directives of the Bible. I continued to struggle intermittently with drug use and pornography. After embarking on my second run at postsecondary education at Valley City State University in North Dakota, I found my resolve to pursue Christ withering in the spiritual vacuum of a secular campus. Somehow, football wasn't as important to me as it had once been. I was missing the company of my family and church friends back home. Within a few months, I slid back into the familiar milieu of substance abuse and promiscuity. However, I was learning that my former lifestyle was like a dissolute city that had become a ghost town. I was unable to find much enjoyment in my old lifestyle. My days were consumed with anger and regret. I was miserable.

I was expelled from the school for fighting and vandalism in May 1999 and wound up in jail on an assault charge. Then, just before I left the state, I injured a man in an altercation at a local bar and fled the state as a fugitive.

It was a disjointed time during which I failed at every endeavor. I moved to Oregon in August to resume my schooling at Southern Oregon University in Ashland. But it was as though I were being chased by all the forces of negativity and self-destruction. I couldn't muster the impetus for any sustained effort. My constant drug use was like a lead overcoat that I couldn't take off. After only a few months, I stopped attending school altogether and drifted like a spirit without a body. For a time, I lived on a couch in a drug house, penniless and despondent. I ran from the pain with whatever intoxicants I could find. My daily goal was to achieve chemically induced oblivion. I frequented local drinking establishments and often got into bar fights. Brushes with the law were a regular occurrence.

In November of 2000, I drove to Seattle to meet with my family. We were to travel to Las Vegas for a Thanksgiving vacation. When I arrived, my mom took one look at me and paled visibly.

She put a hand up to my face. "Peter, what's happened to you?"

I didn't have an answer. My mom later told me, "You

looked horrible in every way." I had two black eyes from a recent altercation. I was feeling a weight of heaviness that I couldn't shake, even in the company of my family.

While we were in Las Vegas, I tried to participate in group activities with my family, but my perpetual need to get loaded kept me away from them for much of the trip. One particularly wild night, I consumed a huge quantity of cocaine and LSD and cavorted around the Strip, completely out of my gourd. Around 5 a.m., I began to come down from the drugs, at which point I started in with dollar margaritas in the casino. At one point, I had a glass in each hand. All I wanted was to pass out.

I had turned a sharp corner in my substance abuse. As if it weren't bad enough that I had long been using drugs as a constant source of pain relief (avoidance), it had come to the point where I used and drank to achieve utter oblivion. It seemed I could no longer enjoy guilt-free consciousness. The way I understood things, my abandonment of God had decisively nullified the grace he had previously extended to me. It was as though God had reached spectacularly into my life and laid heavenly jewels into my hand, which I had allowed to slip through my fingers. My retreat back into dissolute living, which had taken me further down into darkness than ever, seemed to have negated everything positive that had taken place before. I knew too much about God's righteous requirements to entertain the notion that I could somehow still qualify for membership in the ranks of the faithful. To be one of the faithful, you had to be ... *faithful,*

I thought. But my whole life had become a caricature of the failed disciple. I was plagued by feelings of dread. What was left for me? Only the dubious consolation prize of drug-induced forgetfulness.

"It is what it is," I said to myself as I tilted the frozen concoction into my mouth.

Then, suddenly, I heard a voice. It seemed to be issuing from just above my head, even as I stood in the middle of the casino floor. All around me people were laughing, cursing, crying, arguing. There was loud music and the burbling of electronics and coins clattering in the trays. But the voice in my head was perfectly audible, and the gentle kindness in it pierced my heart.

"My son, I love you, and I want to forgive you."

Somehow, I knew without hesitation that it was God speaking. His voice instantly shattered the lies I had been carrying around for years like bullets in my flesh: I had disappointed God, sinned too many times and he could never forgive me, and even if he could forgive me, I could never make it as a Christian. In a moment, I saw the absurd fallacy in these statements that I had recited to myself so often.

In the moments afterward, I became aware that I was completely sober. My mind was as clear as if I'd never drunk a drop of liquor in my life. I could scarcely keep from crying as I made my way up to my hotel room. Once there, I fell to the floor in tears of repentance and cried out to God. My rogue mission was over. I felt a great weight of guilt and dread lift off me.

The next day, my mother and I wept together as I shared the previous evening's events with her. I asked if I could move home and work on my relationship with God. She and my father agreed, and in the following days and weeks, a whole new life began to unfold for me.

☞☞☞

In September of 2001, I entered a year-long term at the Northwind School of Ministry, both to prepare for a life of ministry and to become fully grounded in my Christian faith. The year was difficult and strange and beautiful — a patchwork of experiences that shaped me, even as it revealed God's hand in my life. It was a time of healing and growth. I was not immune to missteps, but God was endlessly patient. In retrospect, I can see how he went about replacing the blunders of my past with good plans for my future. In the classic divine exchange, I was trading my sorrows and broken devices for a new life of health and spiritual vitality. The testing and difficulties I faced were a way for God to remake me. I scarcely resembled the man I had been before.

Nothing in that first year, however, could prepare me for the encounter with God I was to have toward the end of it.

I was in Kansas City attending a conference when it happened. I had been seeking God with a hunger that I had never before experienced or thought possible. One day, as I sat on my couch deep in prayer, I felt the presence of Jesus so strongly that it was as though a flesh-and-blood person was sitting on the couch next to me. I could almost feel the cushions being displaced by his weight. His voice was clearer and more spiritually charged than anything I have experienced before or since. During the prayer, I sang a song. It was new to me, like perhaps the Lord and I invented it on the spot:

> Looking at your face,
> I will never be the same.
> Gazing in your eyes,
> I am filled with Spirit fire.

In the middle of the prayer, I had an experience that, as unreal as it may sound, felt absolutely real to me. It was like Jesus and I were friends, with him sharing a humorous moment from the conference that day: "Do you remember how the speaker's shoe kept coming untied? Once, he thought he'd retied it, but the second he straightened up to go back to the lectern, the laces were already flopping around again." I heard the Lord laughing as he talked about it. I had spotted the same thing and stifled my own laughter while it was happening at the conference. I marveled at the thought that it had tickled God, too!

That prayer sent me into a long season of fasting and seeking God that I would otherwise never have found the grace to undertake. I was so wound up afterward that I took a vow of the ancient Nazarites, who wanted to demonstrate their desire to be closer to God by not shaving or cutting their hair. I did this for a year. I started fasting as though it were pleasant to go without food. One of the fasts lasted 40 days. Picture a man who has always loved to eat, who has been overweight for much of his life, denying himself even a single bite of food for six weeks! While I was on that fast, I happened to be living next door to my grandmother, who told me, "Peter, you have to eat. You're going to die!" She would bring over lemon-meringue pies to try to tempt me off the fast.

The experience I had that day in Kansas City shaped the entire year that followed, during which habitual sins slid off me like vapor. The year 2003 was the first full year since I was 10 that alcohol or drugs never once touched my lips. Later that same year, I came on staff at Northwind. The following year, I became the director of the school and married Jessica, the love of my life, who has since given me three fine boys, Bradley, Joseph and Quinn. In November 2008, I was asked to help found a ministry to help people struggling with substance abuse. Today, I serve in the executive ranks of this same ministry, which last year enrolled 160 clients seeking freedom from the bondage of addiction. During the same year, we provided free sober support groups for 1,300 individuals. The facility has become a frontline infirmary for lost and suffering people. Our services are outpacing most Alaska recovery programs in long-term efficacy.

My life is full of the rewards of service. I feel gratitude and humility as I look back on my troubled years, the intervention of God, the years of plowing and growth and the astonishing season of harvest I am now enjoying. God has authored all of it out of the ashes of my former depravity. Surely humanity's weakness is great, but the love and grace of God is greater.

CONCLUSION

My heart is full. When I became a pastor, my desire was to change the world. My hope was to see people encouraged and the hurting filled with hope. As I read this book, I saw that passion being fulfilled. However, at Northgate Alaska, rather than being content with our past victories, we are spurred to believe that many more can occur.

Every time we see another changed life, it increases our awareness that God really loves people and he is actively seeking to change lives. Think about it: How did you get this book? We believe you read this book because God brought it to you seeking to reveal his love to you. Whether you're a man or a woman, a slope worker or a waitress, blue collar or no collar, a parent or a student, we believe God came to save you. He came to save us. He came to save them. He came to save all of us from the hellish pain we've wallowed in and offer real joy and the opportunity to share in real life that will last forever through faith in Jesus Christ.

Do you have honest questions that such radical change is possible? It seems too good to be true, doesn't it? Each of us at Northgate Alaska warmly invites you to come and check out our church family. Freely ask questions, examine our statements, see if we're "for real" and, if you choose, journey with us at whatever pace you are comfortable. You will find that we are far from perfect. Our scars and sometimes open wounds are still healing, but we just want you to know God is still completing the process of authentic life change in us. We still make mistakes in our journey, like everyone will. Therefore, we acknowledge our continued need for each other's forgiveness and support. We need the love of God just as much as we did the day before we believed in him.

If you are unable to be with us, yet you intuitively sense you would really like to experience such a life change, here are some basic thoughts to consider. If you choose, at the end of this conclusion, you can pray the suggested prayer. If your prayer genuinely comes from your heart, you will experience the beginning stages of authentic life change, similar to those you have read about.

How does this change occur?

Recognize that what you're doing isn't working. Accept the fact that Jesus desires to forgive you for your bad decisions and selfish motives. Realize that without this forgiveness, you will continue a life separated from God and his amazing love. In the Bible, the book of Romans, chapter 6, verse 23 reads, "The result of sin (seeking our way rather than God's way) is death, but the gift that God freely gives is everlasting life found in Jesus Christ."

Believe in your heart that God passionately loves you and wants to give you a new heart. Ezekiel 11:19 reads, "I will give them singleness of heart and put a new spirit within them. I will take away their stony, stubborn heart and give them a tender, responsive heart" (NLT).

Believe in your heart that "if you confess with your mouth that Jesus is Lord and believe in your heart that God raised him from the dead, you will be saved" (Romans 10:9 NLT).

Believe in your heart that because Jesus paid for your failure and wrong motives, and because you asked him to forgive you, he has filled your new heart with his life in such a way that he transforms you from the inside out. Second Corinthians 5:17 reads, "When someone becomes a Christian, he becomes a brand new person inside. He is not the same anymore. A new life has begun!"

Why not pray now?

Lord Jesus, if I've learned one thing in my journey, it's that you are God and I am not. My choices have not resulted in the happiness I hoped they would bring. Not only have I experienced pain, I've also caused it. I know I am separated from you, but I want that to change. I am sorry for the choices I've made that have hurt myself, others and denied you. I believe your death paid for my sins, and you are now alive to change me from the inside out. Would you please do that now? I ask you to come and live in me so that I can sense you are here with me. Thank you for hearing and changing me. Now please help me know when you are talking to me, so I can cooperate with your efforts to change me. Amen.

Wasilla's unfolding story of God's love is still being written ... and your name is in it.

I hope to see you this Sunday!

Dennis Hotchkiss
Northgate Alaska
Wasilla, Alaska

We would love for you to join us at Northgate Alaska!

We meet Sunday mornings at 9 and 11 a.m. at
Teeland Middle School
2788 N Seward Meridian Parkway
Wasilla, AK 99654.

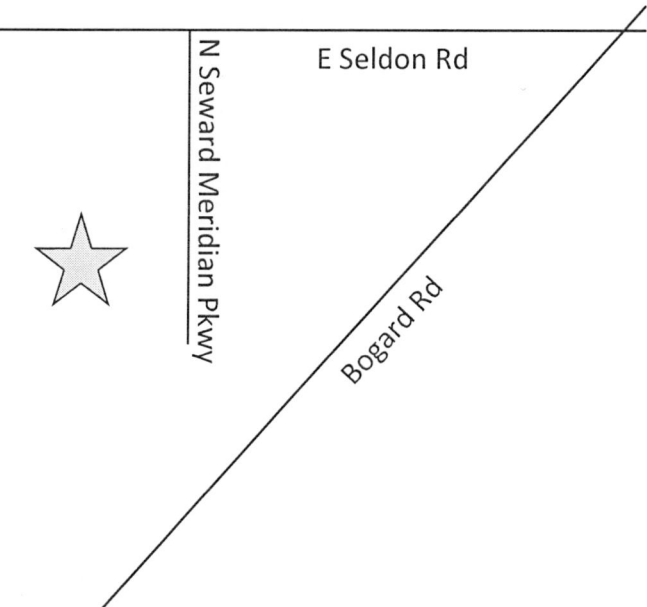

Please call us at 907.864.6701 for directions,
or contact us at www.northgatealaska.com.

For more information on reaching your city with stories from your church, please contact Good Catch Publishing at www.goodcatchpublishing.com

GOOD CATCH
PUBLISHING

Did one of these stories touch you?
Did one of these real people move you to tears?
Tell us (and them) about it on our reader blog at www.goodcatchpublishing.blogspot.com.